LOSING YOUR DOG

To my Dog Allért

"In the course of my work" says Mickie Gustafson, "I have encountered the whole spectrum of sorrow and joy. I have come across anxiety, fear. . . . total confusion and helplessness. But I have also encountered openness and trust and generously shared personal experiences — all of which have contributed to make this book possible."

Mickie Gustafson

LOSING YOUR DOG

Coping with Grief when a Pet Dies

Translated from the Swedish by
Kjersti Board

Illustrated by Britt Lindhè

BERGH

BERGH PUBLISHING, INC.
276 Fifth Avenue, New York, N.Y. 10001

Table of Contents

Introduction

In the course of my work as psychologist and dog specialist I have encountered the whole spectrum of sorrow and joy. Even though we are aware of the painful separation which awaits us at some point in the future, the happiness of owning a dog and the friendship of a dog are enough to make most of us ignore it.

This is a book about the thoughts, feelings and experiences of a dog owner faced with the loss of a faithful and loved companion. The book applies equally to those who have lost a cat or another pet.

In the midst of sorrow and grief there is almost always joy and gratefulness for the past and usually the expressed hope of a new relationship and commitment.

I have come across anxiety, fear and silence, and sometimes also the feeling of total confusion and helplessness that may seize people in the darkest moments in life. But I have also encountered openness and trust and generously shared personal experiences — all of which have contributed to making this book possible.

My heartfelt thanks to all of you!

I hope that those of you who love your pet may find this book useful — those of you who know that the time to say goodbye will come one day.

Mickie Gustafson

Losing Someone You Love

"Tim had been the darling of everyone in the family for ten years. Everybody adored him. He was always happy and friendly, and his antics were a source of joy. He was full of energy, and it was usually he who got the children started — not the other way around.

Since we spent most of our time in each other's company, Tim had become a natural part of my life. I always felt relaxed and harmonious around him. Ours was a very special relationship. A wordless companionship where we just WERE.

The years with Tim added so much both to my own life and to that of my children. He came to be an important part of their upbringing. Thanks, to him they soon learnt to respect and take responsibility for another being. I am convinced that this is one reason why all my children have developed a special tenderness towards all living things.

They learnt early to show their feelings and to care for both animals and people. They were taught that a dog does not exist simply to show us devotion and for us to pet. It also has to be well treated and cared for. It is not only a question of receiving, you have to give something in return.

When Tim died our lives changed. Our days were different. Even though we are a large family, our house was empty and silent. Even though we were thoroughly prepared, it was still hard to come to terms with.

I was very shaken as I drove home from the vet. I have to admit that I was clearly an unsuitable and dangerous driver. I still do not quite remember how I made it home. But I do know that I was unable to go inside the house for several hours.

The first time was horrible. Everybody cried and the talk revolved constantly about Tim. I even woke up at night imagining that I heard him. It is actually not until recently that we have stopped thinking and talking about him all the time. It still happens whenever we visit a place where we used to go together.

Thank God there were many of us to share the grief. It was important to have the opportunity to discuss what had happened, and to know that we were not alone after all. Even though having a family to consider when you yourself were so depressed was hard at times, it was still a comfort not to have to be alone.

Nor did our friends and relatives really understand how we felt and how hard it was on us. If anything, they tried to belittle our sorrow.

You must be allowed to talk. It is absolutely necessary. Empathy feels good, while being ignored is like a slap in the face. It is obviously important, however, that others are sensitive to how much or how long you are willing to talk.

At the vet, I was given as much support and information as the situation warranted, and as I was able to assimilate at the time. I think that it was good that the veterinarian did not remove all hope all at once but actually tried to help and treat Tim. But when he finally realized that there was nothing else he could do, it was equally important that I was told this, frankly and honestly. He explained in detail that there was nothing more to do and also why it would be unfair to Tim to delay our parting too long. He asked me to think it over thoroughly and talk to my family. It was important for us to be allowed to discuss the difficult decision during a period of three or four weeks.

Now, all of a sudden, Tim's life was in our hands. It felt terrible.

We felt guilty about maybe having allowed him to suffer too long. And we felt tremendous anxiety about having to take the irrevocable step. When we finally did what had to be done, we knew that we were doing the right thing. That was our only consolation.

It was an incredibly painful period; nevertheless, I think it was valuable. I had time to talk to the veterinarian and to my family and to prepare myself. After all, we were lucky not to lose Tim suddenly and unexpectedly.

Being present when he was put away was heart-rending, but I still do not wish it otherwise. I wanted to be with him. He felt safe in my company. And to me, it felt natural to give him this last sense of security. I neither wanted, nor was able, to desert him at this point after everything he had given us. That feeling gave me the strength needed to give him as calm, loving and dignified an end as possible.

The personnel at the clinic was fantastic. They helped me by conveying a sense of calm and understanding that warmed my heart. They were not in any hurry, but took their time, and showed their compassion and sympathy in a thousand ways.

Tim was cremated and has been buried. The funeral was important. He was, after all, a beloved member of the family and should not be dispatched in any old way. We do not differentiate emotionally between people and animals when they are alive, so why should we after death?

The delay before his funeral was naturally difficult. But now he is resting in a place where he spent most of his time while alive, and that feels right to us.

We have now accepted that Tim is no longer with us. Even if we still miss him very much — and we must be allowed to feel this way — life does, after all, continue.

One day, when we feel ready and prepared, we will welcome another dog into our family, and it will become a source of joy and harmony. Not in the same way as Tim, of course — but in a different and maybe equally rewarding way."

A Severed Bond

The above was the beautiful and sensitive account of a friend who prefers to remain anonymous. Her loving words are probably representative of many who have lost a beloved dog and undergone a similar grieving process.

And even if another dog eventually will brighten the life of the family, the memory of Tim will still always remain in their hearts.

Those who have themselves been very close to an animal are able to understand and relate to the feelings of grief and emptiness that accompany the death of a much loved pet. Those who never have experienced the emotional bonds which sometimes develop between a human being and an animal will obviously find it more difficult to understand the extent of this loss and the emotional upheaval that it provokes. Some think that a dead dog can be replaced by a new one right away, the way you replace a car or change a shirt.

But a dead animal is more than just a dead body. It represents happiness that has been lost and a bond that has been severed. Harmony is suddenly missing, and a wonderful source of happiness is no more. The resulting feeling of loneliness may feel overwhelming and almost unbearable. It is the end of friendship and love, which cannot ever totally be replaced.

The Nature of Grief

Death is as natural to existence as birth — this we realize intellectually. We also know that loss is accompanied by a period of intense grief, anxiety and feeling of loneliness. But even though we know this, we are never quite emotionally prepared for it.

Although sorrow does not admit of any shortcuts, it need not entail total confusion and chaos when it strikes. If we try to understand the nature and various stages of the grieving process, we will be able to deal with it and overcome it more readily. We do not have to be the totally exposed and helpless victims of our emotions.

Grief is a state of psychological crisis. The word "crisis" is Greek, meaning a decisive turn of events, sudden change or fatal disturbance. Crises in life are necessary to our personal development and increased self-awareness. But crises, at their worst, may also lead to lifelong suffering.

We must always bear in mind that grief changes, however, and that if we work hard we will be able to overcome it completely.

The common denominator of all crises is that you find yourself exposed to events and feelings that are so different and so powerful that you have a hard time mastering the situations that arise. Grief is an example of such an extreme state of stress which may absorb us for a short period or for a long time, dominating our whole personality.

The pre-eminent characteristics of grief are anxiety provoked by loss and a yearning for the departed which may at times assume physical proportions.

Every separation or crisis entails a deep, at times overwhelming, sense of abandonment and loneliness. These feelings are common to everybody undergoing some form of crisis.

The Grieving Pet Owner

A pet is never self-sufficient in the same way as a wild animal living in nature. Throughout its life, a pet is dependent on a human to care for it. And many people do indeed lavish all sorts of love and care on their pets.

When they acquire a puppy, they eagerly seek all kinds of expert advice to help them satisfy the physical and psychological needs of the puppy in the best possible way. The puppy then grows up, and they have many happy — and comfortable — years together.

Time passes, and eventually they come full circle. In the course of the aging process, the dog enters its "second childhood," becoming increasingly dependent on the love and care of his owner. The latter has to pay close attention to the dog's needs regarding diet, exercise, vitamin supplements etc. — just as he did when it was a puppy. The difference is that dog and human have now had time to grow close and form strong bonds of affection.

The little puppy, who once joined the household with a wonderful zest for life, gave rise to great expectations. It made us laugh — and frown — at its endearing clumsiness and antics. That stage is now a thing of the past. It is no longer a young and carefree stranger. Instead, we find ourselves lavishing the greatest possible care on an aged and fragile being whom we have grown attached to and have come to love from the very bottom of our hearts. And at this sensitive stage that we are separated . . .

What use is it then knowing from the beginning that the lifespan of a dog is shorter than our own? And what is the use of common sense? Love was never a part of common sense.

Many fail to take into account — which is only human — that the being they are lavishing such tender loving care on is "only a dog." They give of their love, without reservation, never pausing to consider that their loving care will one day be cut short and be replaced by vast, terrifying silence.

Studies have shown that the hardest loss of all is the loss of a child. Dogs and children are obviously two different things, but there are nevertheless some similarities — first and foremost our own attitude. There are those — and they are many — who love and care for their pet with the same affection and involvement as they once loved or might love a child. This does obviously not mean that they treat their pets as if they were human.

They simply love. To them, it is perfectly natural that love might appear in different guises. To them, their loss may be excruciatingly difficult to endure. They are facing a period of intense grief and have every right to our sympathy and understanding.

The Different Stages of Grief

Studies of adults and children show that grief usually adheres to a distinct pattern, which may be divided into four different stages: shock, reaction, working through and re-direction.

The different stages are not always separate and distinct. Occasionally a stage may be omitted or intermingled with another.

Shock

The stage of shock may last only a short time or up to several weeks. During this stage there is a strong denial of reality. You either do not want or are unable to understand what has happened. You may appear calm on the outside, but inside there is only confusion and chaos. During the stage of shock you feel almost stunned; you don't feel anything, you don't understand anything. You do not pay attention to what is being said and find it difficult to make decisions.

A dog owner who is being told that his or her dog has a serious illness is often subjected to abnormal stress and is unable to think. In this state, he may be forced to make decisions on whether to have the dog euthanized. Decisions made in this emotional state may obviously be ill-considered.

In that situation, the main concern is usually that the dog not be allowed to suffer needlessly, which is why the decision to have the dog put to sleep is often taken too hastily. It is not until later that you may begin to question whether the decision was the right one. And then it is too late. These doubts may haunt the dog owner for a long time.

It is therefore of utmost importance that the owner avoid making this kind of decisions during this state — provided that it can be done without inflicting further unnecessary suffering on the dog.

The affected person may often be outwardly calm, but beneath the surface all is chaos. Afterwards, he may find it hard to remember what was said or done. It is important that those who dispense medical information are aware of this. Crucial information is too often imparted at the same time as a profoundly shocking message, with the consequence that it has minimal effect and the information is forgotten.

Johan Cullberg

Reaction and Grief Management

The reaction stage begins the moment you clearly realize what has happened or is about to happen. You understand what has occurred, but not why. You keep trying to find a meaning and ultimate reason for what has taken place.

Since grief is also to a large extent physical, it is not uncommon to experience a number of physical symptoms during this period, such as headaches, sleeplessness, tiredness, stomach problems, loss of appetite, compulsive snacking and weight gain.

When you ask dog owners about their reactions during the period immediately following the death of their dog, they usually tell you that the dog was constantly in their thoughts, that they felt restless and anxious, that they had a hard time concentrating on their daily tasks, and that they found it difficult to get involved in their work.

Many also say that — against all reason — they were forever looking for their dog or listening for various sounds or signs of it. This is because their sense of loss is so overwhelming that it simply dominates normal logical thinking.

This watchfulness also means that you become more and more sensitive to everything that might remind you of the dead pet. You listen and look, expecting to see or hear the missing dog — and sometimes it seems to you that you do. All your senses are on the alert and receptive to everything that might be a sign of communication from the dead animal. And this — the momentary impression of seeing or hearing what you are looking for — provides both solace and a respite in your search.

Others strive to forget and try to erase the dead pet and the tragedy from their thoughts. This reaction is less common, however. Most try to retain as clear a memory of the dog as possible, along with the sense that he is still around.

Those who do not believe that life is over when the body dies find it somewhat easier to cope with their grief. Others find consolation in the thought that the dog is happy now, it does not have to suffer, that it has had a long and satisfying life, etc.

In your confusion and search for temporary relief by looking for someone who no longer exists, you often tend to overlook life and the companionship that your surroundings have to offer. You feel as if you have lost the most important thing in life. What is left seems oddly unreal and irrelevant.

Another characteristic of this period is exaggerated anger and irritation.

Those who try to persuade a grieving person that it is futile to mourn and to look to the future instead may well encounter irritation and unkindness or even agressiveness.

In searching for meaning — and maybe chiefly for understanding — you may have a hard time accepting the fact that life causes us so much pain, seemingly for no reason. You try at all cost to find an explanation. Was the doctor or the veterinarian or the animal handler at fault? Did you really do everything in your power?

Your anger may sometimes also be directed against the pet itself who "deserted you and let you down." Thoughts like these are rarely long-lived, however, the anger turning to guilt instead about thoughts, feelings or reaction.

This seemingly unwarranted anger may wax and wane by turns, often culminating during the first month. Depression, withdrawal and apathy alternate with periods of anger. Your zest for life is just about gone. The grieving person withdraws and has no urge to participate in life.

The dog owner may make the veterinarian the scapegoat. The anger of those who lose a young dog tends to be greater, and is frequently directed at the vet. There are obviously cases when it is justified, but it can also be an expression of the need to find someone to blame in the case of the death of a young dog.

Not all dog owners vent their unhappiness openly, however. It may be hidden behind phrases like "it was nice of the vet to get up in the middle of the night to put my dog to sleep." "I was afraid to ask any more questions since the vet seemed ill at ease." "I didn't know how much of the vet's time I could waste." "I didn't want to be a bother, the vet had other things to see to."

Guilt feelings are understandable and extremely common in the course of the grief process. These feelings are almost always unfounded, however — a fact which the bereaved eventually comes to realize.

Guilt feelings may be caused by the fact that you yourself had to make the decision to have the dog euthanized. You start wondering whether it was the right decision, or whether you should have waited a while, or tried another form of treatment or seen another veterinarian.

Others blame themselves for waiting too long to have the dog put away, even though it may have been ill and feeble for a long time.

Re-orientation

Your thoughts and preoccupation with the dead dog naturally fade after a while. Search, anger, guilt feelings and even the sense of loss diminish little by little, and life returns to normal.

To part is "to die a little." Someone who has been a large part of your life will obviously leave a great void. But eventually you

feel the urge to see this void filled. Life starts calling you again, and you will give in to your longing and zest for life.

Grief remains as a scar in our consciousness. But it does not prevent us from participating in life and rejoicing in it. Crises are a part of our existence that has to be accepted.

Time may not heal all wounds, but it does help us forget acute pain. We will never forget someone close. But our ability to forget pain may make us risk hoping for a new relationship.

Summary

- You will never fully be able to emotionally anticipate a loss. But you may learn to comprehend the nature of it, and thus be better prepared to handle it than you otherwise would have been. You don't have to become a helpless victim, totally at the mercy of your feelings.

- Those who experience great grief share an overwhelming sense of desertion and loneliness, as well as a yearning for the deceased, which may become almost unbearable at times.

- Grief has a purely physical dimension in which the body responds with more or less pronounced stress symptoms such as headaches, sleeplessness, loss of appetite, stomach problems, etc.

- Life appears unreal and meaningless to a grieving person, who may often become apathetic and deeply depressed. Guilt feelings are followed by anger at the injustice of life.

- Guilt feelings may appear especially heavy and oppressive in the case of pet owners, since they are often responsible for having made the decision to have the dog put away.

Factors Influencing Grief

They were my neighbors for many years, and I met them almost every day. Both reminded me of characters out of a story book: the owner with a long grey beard and a little red nose and the dog, shaggy and grey with almond-shaped eyes. They actually resembled each other, both silver-grey, with bright, twinkling eyes.

They had lived in the house for as long as I could remember. I guess that I thought that they would always be there, adding a beautiful and unreal touch to our bustling street. For they were truly beautiful. Not just because they transmitted the special wisdom and beauty of old age, but also because they conveyed a sense of harmony and blessed calm, so rare in our frenzied time. I never grew tired of this silvery couple.

We often stopped and chatted a little while. But even though I watched them age, I never considered the possibility that one day they would be gone for good.

Then one day I encountered the old man without his dog. He

was sitting alone on a park bench, more unearthly than ever. From his vacant look and the way he slumped I realized immediately what had happened. I sat down on the bench, and we sat there next to each other for a long while without uttering a word, absorbed in our own thoughts. Then he lifted his head and slowly started to talk. I will never forget his words.

— It is actually not sad, only very lonely. It is hard when we no longer can touch them or see them. Even so, I know that Silver hasn't really left me.

I did not doubt his words. His eyes were lit by an inner light and a faith that silenced all doubts.

I looked over at my own dog, at the moment absorbed in following the progress of an ant across one of his hind paws. It was a form of pursuit that he appeared to deem appropriate for a dog of his years.

In my heart I hoped to share some of the old man's wisdom myself when the difficult day would arrive in my life. And I knew that it was not too far off.

Six months later the old man was no more. But in my mind, the bench where we talked on that occasion is still bathed in a silvery light today.

Resignation and Acceptance

Grief may be experienced in so many different ways. It may be brief or long, immediate or delayed.

Older people usually react to grief differently from young people. An old person, seasoned by many setbacks in life, bears his loss with a resigned acceptance and maybe with deeper insight.

But in all cases, grief must run its course. The grieving process may sometimes last for quite a long time, occasionally as much as a couple of years. The memories and the grief may sometimes become quite obtrusive, even after quite some time has passed.

Repression and Denial

Most people respond to an acute crisis with some kind of "delaying" defense mechanism which helps them approach painful reality a little at a time.

One way to protect yourself and to avoid pain is to repress or deny as long as possible what lies ahead or what has already taken place.

There is no denying that the lifespan of a dog is shorter than that of a human being. But even if you obviously know this, it is still something that many pet owners fail to accept consciously and which they repress.

A surprising number of those who lose aged dogs are unprepared when the death occurs. One woman told me that she wished she had had her dog buried, but that the dog had died so suddenly and unexpectedly that she had not had time to think the matter through and consider her options.

The dog was more than fourteen when it died!

Death and separation is something that we humans do not like to think or speak about. A dog owner is no exception.

Age and Gender of Dog Owner

The age and gender of the owner is another important factor in the reaction to the death of a dog.

The reaction of a child or a young person is often spontaneous and violent. They are almost inconsolable in their grief. A grown-up is more matter-of-fact in his way of dealing with bereavement. He or she may be in the midst of a demanding job situation that may mean that the sorrow has to be set aside, at least for the time being.

The grief of an old person is more tempered. Those who have accepted the transitory nature of life and who have stopped fighting it are able to face painful situations more calmly and objectively.

Women and men usually express their grief in different ways. A study of the reactions of those who have lost their partners indicates that women usually do not fare as well as men. The loss is more deeply felt, because men occupy a more central position in the thoughts of women than the other way round. Even though sex stereotypes are changing, it is still the role — and the privilege — of the female to be more emotional.

The grief of a man may be every bit as intense as that of a woman, but he is usually more limited when it comes to expressing it. This is partly because of his perception of what is expected of him, but it is also the result of acquired inhibitions when it comes to expressing strong emotions.

Emotional Involvement

The more central someone is to somebody else, the more time they have spent together, the deeper the emotional involvement, affection, security and dependence that characterize the relationship, the harder the separation.

A dog is always there. Every single day. Always trusting. Always happy and friendly. Trivial little events, hardly noticeable, have assured the dog of a very important role and function in the life of his owner. It may be a little pat in passing, earning a wag of the tail or a lick in return, habitual greetings, walks, food rituals, companionship in front of the TV, etc.

Owning a dog also confers a very special identity on you — that of being a dog owner. Since this only accounts for a small part of the total identity of a human, it may be thought to be unimportant. But it is not. Having a dog entails a very special lifestyle, a way of living. This becomes evident to the owner when the dog dies, if not before. A lot of little routines and events are suddenly missing. Responsibilities which formerly might have been thought to be burdensome now leave a big void. It is not only the bond with the dog that is broken but also that with other dog owners.

Many grow so close to their dogs over the years that they start talking in terms of "us" and "we." They mention their name and that of the dog in one breath — they simply belong together. When the dog is gone, they lose a vital and living part of their own identity. Those who have incorporated the dog in their own identity this intimately, almost perceiving the dog as part of themselves, obviously experience the loss as extremely painful.

This is one of the reasons why many feel that they cannot live without a dog. They acquire another one almost as soon as they lose the first one. That way they keep their identity and go on with their usual life.

However, those who never thought of themselves as having these strong emotional ties to their dog sometimes discover — to their great surprise — that they grieve much more than expected. Unbeknownst to them, the dog had insinuated itself into their emotions and brought them more joy than they ever knew. This they discover once the dog is gone.

Preparatory Anxiety

The surviving owner's reactions are affected by the circumstances surrounding the death, the possible warning signs and whether he had a chance to prepare for the approaching loss.

Premature death, for instance the loss of a child or someone in the flower of youth, causes the most serious and severe disturbance. Accepting the quiet death of an old person is far different from the tragic snuffing of a young life. The sudden and unexpected death of a child affords us no chance to prepare ourselves. Even with all the warning in the world it would still be hard to prepare for the coming grief.

Preparatory anxiety work prepares the mourner both intellectually and emotionally for the day when the loss will become a fact. Anxiety work is based on anticipation. It is a way of preparing for what is in store and the possible consequences. Anxiety work enables us to alter our expectations of the future little by little, and to go through, ahead of time, the emotions that the loss will entail.

There are also certain differences between those who lose older dogs as opposed to those who lose young ones.

In the former category, few want a new dog right away, while the others often acquire another dog before long. The loss of an old dog, one that you have lived with for a number of years, obviously leaves a greater void. Therefore you require more time to work through your grief.

The dog may have become such an important part of your life that a new one would contrast too sharply with what used to be. You do not have the strength, so you let it ride for a while. A certain amount of preparatory anxiety may ensure that those who lose an older dog will be less panic-stricken and better prepared, and therefore will refrain from getting a new dog right away.

To many, preparatory work may be the hardest part of the grieving process. Whether the anxiety work is conscious or unconscious it may result in the same physical and psychological symptoms as the actual grief process. The problems may range from the purely practical to deep-seated anxieties.

A dog who is getting old and feeble reminds the observant owner that death is inevitable, and that the time to say goodbye is drawing near. You are no longer able to take as long walks as before. The dog requires more rest, greater care, and maybe a special diet and medicine. Active outdoor life gradually decreases. You may find yourself spending more and more quiet evenings at home instead of gathering mushrooms or skiing.

The net effect, whether you admit it or not, is that you are reminded of something that you subconsciously are trying to keep at a distance. To many dog owners, this is a painful period. What lies ahead is nothing you look forward to with eagerness. Nor is it anything that you ultimately can change.

This may be a period of mounting anxiety and feeling of helplessness. Some react by embarking on the grief process more or less consciously. They may therefore show signs of early grief, depression, listlessness, confusion, weight gain or loss, disquiet, restlessness, etc. long before the dog is dead or has started to show the usual signs of old age. The hardest thing for many during this period, is uncertainty and helplessness and sometimes also the unfamiliarity with their own reactions.

If you don't know with any degree of certainty what is in store for you, you will have a hard time understanding why you are not feeling well.

Besides, the dog is demonstrably still alive! It is difficult to admit to yourself and to others that you have already begun to mourn your dog.

To those who have gone through such thorough preparatory anxiety, the death of the dog may actually prove a relief! Finally your grief is "real." All your pain is now allowed to surface. No more passive waiting for the inevitable fatal blow. What you dreaded has come to pass and nothing can get worse. Waiting and waiting, knowing the outcome, is worse. Preparatory anxiety work may lay the groundwork for a calmer, but not necessarily less painful, grieving process.

Those who lose a young dog are in the midst of active dog ownership. It is obviously a great blow to lose a dog at that stage. It is a shock, there seems to be no discernable reason, a commitment which was begun was never really concluded. In such a situation, you may be tempted to get a new dog as soon as possible.

The Situation of the Bereaved

Your ability to handle your grief is naturally affected by whatever crises may coincide with the death of your dog. Things like a difficult teenage crisis, menopause, unemployment or the threat of impending divorce further add to your burden.

The more losses that occur simultaneously, the more difficult the grief. A woman who had lost her husband six months before the death of her dog evidenced more grief at the dog's death than at her husband's. It was not that the dog was more important to her than the husband, but her grief had now doubled.

Being alone, with no one to confide in, having to return to an empty home with no one to welcome you obviously makes for a more difficult grief process than having a family or close friends in the background for support. If everyone shared a close relationship to the deceased, they will find a strong sense of community in their grief.

There used to be more rituals surrounding death. There is less emphasis on the religious ceremony (the funeral), resulting in the weakening of an important means of expressing sorrow and farewell.

The funeral is important to the closest mourners, providing an accepted way of displaying grief. It may be comforting to have friends and relatives around to share your grief. You are not alone. In some instances, the funeral may be the only opportunity for venting grief and loneliness openly and without inhibition.

The dog owner usually does not have this opportunity, and some do not find it necessary. However, many actually claim that they miss a funeral as a step in the recovery process towards a life without a dog. Some therefore opt for having their dog cremated or buried. Others put a white cloth on the table, put out flowers and light a candle before a picture of the dog.

People devise their own mourning rituals in different ways. Sometimes it is done furtively and with a sense of shame, even though it is the undisputed right of everyone to be allowed to mourn without incurring the ridicule of the surroundings. Many state that it feels wrong to have to give up the dog's remains just like that.

Tears, frustration and sorrow may be wrongly perceived as weakness and lack of self-control instead of as a psychological necessity.

A woman who does not cry at her husband's funeral is thought to be in control of herself. Parents who lose a child, but who go on with their lives without excessive manifestations of grief, are considered strong and invite great sympathy. This "strength" may be a sign that the bereaved has been taught not to burden others with his grief and suffering. But it may also be a more or less conscious way of trying to avoid pain and anxiety.

— It meant a lot to be allowed to talk about Jeppe, a woman said, about him as a puppy and as old and feeble and about what we had gone through together . . . I had a constant need to talk about him for several weeks and months after his death. He was the only thing I wanted to talk about during this dreadful period. I could keep it up for hours on end. Everything else seemed unimportant and unreal. Repeating the same things over and over, crying and airing my feelings and my grief finally undid the tight knots. I was lucky to have a friend who was understanding and who gave of herself and of her time. I owe her a great debt of gratitude. She herself had gone through the same grief as I.

If sorrow is not expressed in words, it will freeze. Talking about the loved one, expressing your feelings and finding a ready listener is therefore a very important part of all grief work. Those who live in social isolation or who come up against people who carry on unfeelingly and cheerfully as if nothing had happened may feel incredibly lonely, unhappy and deserted.

Guilt and grief are a double burden. Guilt feelings, justified or not, may be treated by your surroundings in a similar uncaring way. Thinking that he may ease your pain, an outsider may try to belittle the guilt feelings of the bereaved. Expressions such as "don't think about it," "you did what you could," or "it wasn't your fault" may be true and perfectly justified, but still be taken as a kind of evasiveness

---

Grief is treated as if it were a weakness, a lack of self-discipline, a reprehensible and bad habit instead of a psychological necessity.

Geoffrey Gorer

that is of no help to the bereaved. He or she is unable to accept such assurances or explanations. What is needed is a fellow human-being taking time to listen.

Summary

- Repression is a common way of protecting yourself from painful experiences. You are unable to face the extent of your loss right away.

- The more love, the more dependence, the more affection and security in a relationship the harder the separation.

- Being alone, having no one to talk to, returning to an empty and deserted home makes the grief especially hard to bear. We all need someone to lean on when things are bad.

- Funerals and rituals are meaningful and help us in our grief work. The pet owner is no exception, but often hesitates to openly arrange a beautiful farewell ceremony for fear of negative reactions from his surroundings.

- Talking about your grief and loneliness is an important part of the grieving process. The dog owner too often feels that open grief is not allowed and therefore is inhibited in his grieving process.

Let Live or Let Die

Ivan is a sensitive and serious man who regards ownership of a dog as an important and serious commitment. He is the kind of person who never gets carried away or acts impulsively. This does not mean that he is a bore or lacks all feeling. On the contrary, his dry and self-deprecating humor often invites a smile or laughter. In his own straightforward and honest way, he often touches on subjects that we all think of sometimes but never discuss.

Ivan's relationship with his dog Ami was obviously colored by his personality. To begin with, it was not an impulse buy. There were no surprises. Nothing was left to chance.

— Life is full of surprises he said, not least when it comes to dogs, I have noticed. But if you weigh everything carefully from the beginning, you don't have to be sorry later. When it comes to Ami, I now realize that it was probably better this way.

The years went by, and Ami gradually lost her youthful vigor and vitality. She turned into a little grey-haired lady, seemingly as dignified and prudent as her master. Ivan therefore started to prepare for "the dark day," as he called it.

— Ami was sick from time to time. She became the victim of various aches and pains, and we feared they would extinguish the light in her eyes for ever. But, with the help of the vet, she managed to crawl back to life every single time.

But the dark day was approaching — and her master knew it. One day, Ami suddenly became very ill. They quickly took her to the vet. Ivan obviously hoped that she would recover once more. This is how he describes what happened:

— As always, when something was the matter with Ami, I was beside myself with worry. Even so, I tried to look at things realistically, although I think my common sense failed me this time. Something in Ami's eyes made me suspect that the dark day had come, after all. I remember that I felt curiously disoriented. Ami was breathing very heavily in my arms while I was talking to the vet. I knew right away that he would think it better for Ami if she were allowed to die and not prolong her pain. "She is old, she is tired and sick, very sick," he said. I looked Ami deeply in the eyes and I too, suddenly felt very tired and very old. I felt drained inside. It was up to me to decide whether Ami was to live or die. I looked helplessly at the vet. I, a sensible grown-up used to making decisions, stood there helpless as a child, appealing to the vet to help me. Seconds went by, minutes went by — and finally I spoke the words. Ami would be allowed to die. She had had a long, and as I think, rather good life. But now it was over. I felt very torn, but steeled myself and clung to the vet's words "She is old, she is tired and sick, very sick." When the whole thing was over, and Ami had fallen asleep in my lap, I left on trembling legs. An unanswered question was nagging me: Did I do the right thing? Had I shown Ami my love? Even today, whenever I put a flower on her grave, I am seized by that anxiety. It is no longer the same remorse and reproaches as before. But for several months after Ami's death, I would be seized by doubts and start to hate myself. Who was I to decide over life and death? Now that I see the whole thing from a greater distance, I realize that I would have reproached myself no matter what I had done. Ami did not have to suffer any more. But to decide whether someone you love should live or die was beyond doubt the hardest decision of my life.

The Difficult Decision

The only thing we can do whenever somebody falls victim to a painful and fatal disease, is to try to make his or her suffering easier — and then wait for life to be extinguished. With an animal we are able to cut short its suffering. Availing ourselves of this option may spell relief for the animal — and also for its owner. But facing the decision of whether to shorten someone's life naturally leads to feelings of extreme anxiety.

It is rather rare that a dog is allowed to die of old age. It is usually so enfeebled by illness that the owner is forced to make this difficult decision sooner or later.

The questions surrounding it are numerous and difficult to answer: Is there a chance that an operation or medication might cure the dog? Is it fair to the dog to have it submit to various treatments just because I find it difficult to say goodbye? Is it not true that every dying or seriously wounded animal — or person — will fight for its life as long as possible? Wouldn't I? Wouldn't I choose life over death, no matter what the price? Is it really up to me to decide over the life or death of someone?

There are no given answers to these and similar questions. No matter what you decide, doubts, self-reproach, anxiety and new questions will follow.

The fact that we view the dog as a family member — which it actually is, in many respects — suggests the depth of this problem. Deciding when someone close to you will die, or actually helping a suffering and incurably ill person to leave this life, is called euthanasia. Sometimes it is also referred to as mercy killing. No matter how much empathy and love is involved, it is still punishable by law.

Deciding on the death of your own dog is perfectly legal, on the other hand. The moral dilemma and the anxiety are still present, however.

The laws against euthanasia protect not only the sick person. The law also protects the next-of-kin from an extremely difficult decision-making process and the inevitable conflicts of conscience afterwards.

There is no such protection for the dog owner. Responsibility for the decision rests squarely on his or her shoulders. At the same time, the pet owner has a freedom of action which, in its way, may be viewed as a positive thing. It is from this perspective that the decision of possible euthanasia must be viewed.

There are obviously no general advice to give to those who face the decision of whether to let their dog live or die. No outsider can say what is right and wrong in an individual case. The ultimate decision is always that of the owner.

There are, however, a number of different factors in the decision-making process that must be taken into account such as the dog's physical and emotional condition, the vet's opinion, your own views, etc.

If the dog is very old and very sick and if it is unlikely to recover, the decision is not so hard as it might otherwise be.

But reality is seldom simple. The dog may be old, and it may have an illness that requires an operation and lengthy convalescence. Then questions arise like: Will the dog survive the operation? If it does, will it recover fully? What is the risk of post-operative complications? Will the period of convalescence be long and difficult? Such

---

I began to feel that the methods of my profession of prolonging lives and curing illness — one of the noblest goals of our civilization — sometimes were more cruel than the ways of Nature itself, where a serious illness soon leads to the liberation of Death . . .

When Stephen, a friend of one of my colleagues, died, I realized acutely that compassion is needed as a counterweight to our medical heroism. Having suffered a serious heart attack, he lay strapped in bed with tubes attached to every orifice. The damage was so severe that a no-resuscitation order was issued, should his heart give out. He cried out with pain and fear, but no one wanted to prescribe painkillers for fear that it would hasten the inevitable and constitute euthanasia.

Finally my colleague had to intervene, even though his friend was officially under somebody else's care. He gave him a shot of Nembutal. After the injection, Stephen was able to relax and leave this world peacefully and quietly. He whispered a silent "thank you" and fell asleep in five minutes.

Bernie S. Siegel

---

considerations are obviously present in the case of young dogs, but they grow more common as the dog gets older.

In case of a seriously ill young dog, the situation might be especially pressing since we find ourselves faced with possibly having to cut short a life that has been too brief.

Time and Money

A sick dog may require much expenditure of both time and money. This may be costlier than you originally thought, and more than you can manage and has to be considered carefully before you subject your dog to surgery. An operation may require constant care afterwards, followed by lengthy medication. To have the dog undergo an operation and then a long and difficult period of convalescence, only to discover that you have neither the time nor the money to give the dog the care it requires, is obviously unfair both to the dog and to yourself.

This is obvious, you may say. But it is not at all obvious that you will know from the beginning exactly what the treatment will entail. Maybe the dog has to be walked more often than usual, maybe it has to be given frequent medication, maybe it has to be watched constantly, etc. Maybe there will be complications entailing intensified aftercare. The cost of the medication may be many times greater than you originally counted on, etc.

This, on top of an already strained budget and/or schedule, may make the situation unnecessarily difficult and can become untenable in the long run.

Quality of Life as Deciding Factor

The most important consideration to most of those who face the decision of possible euthanasia is the dog's quality of life. Does the dog still retain its zest for life, does it function well enough to enjoy life, or is every day a burden?

This is not always easy to see. There are blind and deaf dogs who get along surprisingly well and seem well-adjusted.

I heard about a woman who was told that her four-year old dog, Rapp, was going blind. What should she do? What was the chance that Rapp would enjoy life in the future? It is part of the story that the woman's profession was training seeing-eye dogs for the blind.

If all those blind people, whom I encounter in my job, value and enjoy life, she told herself, why should not Rapp do the same? He, at least, has his well-developed senses of smell and hearing to fall back on.

She opted for letting the dog live. She guided her blind dog — who actually did not need much help — for four years. By staying where it felt at home, it got along surprisingly well. Rapp was still an active and happy dog.

Dogs may develop heart trouble, joint problems, thyroid deficiency, etc. With the help of medication they may still continue to lead a full life free from pain.

Good Days and Bad

Older dogs are obviously prone to all kinds of ailments. Many can be treated medically so that they remain largely free from pain.

Ludde, an eight-year old retriever, is a good example. He had been taking medication for his arthritis for a year. The medicine was able to ease his pain. He had his good days and his bad — just like everyone else of advanced years and who suffers from little aches and pains. He was an active dog, however, with a seemingly undiminished zest for life.

Ali was another eight-year old with similar problems. For some reason, he was unable to tolerate the medication. With or without medication, he kept growing worse. Practically every day was a burden. He did not want to go out. He hardly had the strength to drag himself up a small flight of stairs, and his eyes grew more and more lifeless and dull.

Ali's mistress knew that he would never get well but that, on the contrary, his days would get more and more painful. She decided to let Ali end his life. The period preceding her decision was filled with doubts. One day he seemed a little more alert and did not seem to be in much pain. On those days the thought of euthanasia seemed misplaced. Next day he was so poor and weak that it seemed to be the only thing to do.

This is often the case with older dogs. On good days, you breathe a sigh of relief, hoping for improvement. But bad days are brutal and bitter, and you keep hoping that this is not the end. When the bad days become too frequent, the time is ripe for a decision.

Temper and Aggressiveness

A very sick dog, like a very sick person, is irritable and temperamental, which may cause great problems both for the dog owner and for the surroundings. A dog who is affected by his illness in this way, is hard to have around and is probably himself suffering mentally.

The change in behavior may force you to keep it away from situations and company that it has previously been part of. It may no longer be able to stand noisy children or boisterous company. Either you exclude it, or if it is allowed to be present, it is scolded for behaving badly. Its quality of life has changed for the worse by either being excluded from accustomed activities and company or punished too often.

Jopp is an example of this. He was a mixed breed who started to show increased aggressiveness when he was one year old. His young mistress, who was mainly responsible for his care and training, sought my help in curbing his aggressions.

Jopp's behavior improved considerably after a long and rather strenuous training period. After a while, he began to have a relapse. On good days, he was like most family dogs: affectionate, sweet and good-natured. But he could not stand strangers. He would tolerate them, but they were never welcome. On bad days he would suddenly attack strangers and even persons he knew well.

A veterinarian was consulted and discovered liver damage which could not be cured either through diet or treatment. Jopp lost weight and became more and more irritable. He was shut up more and more often. He had to stay on a leash. Finally they were afraid to let him be among other dogs or people.

His mistress tried desperately to overcome his aggressiveness through training but made too little headway compared to the punishment and isolation he had had to endure. Finally, she reluctantly gave up. It was an extremely hard decision, for Jopp was a young dog. He was her faithful friend, and she had made every effort to allow him to live.

I will never forget her deep despair when she stood outside the veterinary clinic with Jopp's leash in her hand.

— I feel as if I have let him down, she said, even though I know that his life was not a real life. This was finally the only thing I could do for him.

Hurry Slowly

There are different opinions on the right of an animal to its life — and its death. There is a broad spectrum of views, from that of somebody who has his dog put away because it fails to come up to a certain beauty standard, to somebody who can not bear to say goodbye even though the dog is very ill and frail. Both of these extremes view the other as immoral and selfish. Both have little understanding for the actions of the other, but are fully prepared to justify their own.

Here is an example: A man was telling anyone willing to listen about his neighbor's cruelty to animals. His neighbor was an old man who had an aged, infirm dog. The dog had a hard time walking because of a joint problem. Every step seemed to cause pain. The man could not bring himself to have the dog euthanized. Whenever somebody brought the matter up, he looked evasive, quickly gathering up his dog and leaving.

The other neighbor, who had gone on so volubly about what he referred to as cruelty to animals and which he considered the height of selfishness, had himself had two dogs put away within the space of a year. X-rays had revealed that both had had minor hip joint defects. No serious defect, but enough to make him fear that they would not acquit themselves well in a dog show. Neither dog showed the symptoms of any illness, but the man was bent on showing his dogs and did not want to take any chances. His ethical system allowed him to have his dogs euthanized for selfish reasons, while that of his neighbor — for equally selfish reasons — permitted the old dog to live too long. In one case, the dog was forced to live too long and in needless pain. In the other, the dogs were denied any life whatsoever!

When we face the decision of whether a dear friend is to live or die, we may be blinded by our own selfishness and by our emotions.

In such a case, it may be wise to speak to others who understand our feelings, but who may have greater emotional distance and who therefore are more objective.

In addition to family members and friends, you may want to consult your veterinarian. He or she can contribute an objective and factual description of the physical condition of your dog and of its chances for recovery. If you are not satisfied with his opinion, you should not rest until you have talked to yet another veterinarian.

In the final analysis, the decision belongs to the dog's owner. If the dog is neither ill or in great pain, it is always advisable to hurry slowly until you are convinced of what is right.

Preparations

When the decision to have the dog put away has been made, a number of other questions present themselves, for example: How and when should it be done? Is the process painful or traumatic to the dog? Should I make an appointment right away, or should I allow myself yet some time with the dog? Should I be present? Will I be able to take it? Will it make a difference to the dog if I am not there?

By giving careful thought to these questions beforehand you do not have to be unprepared when the day comes for making a decision.

Picking the Right Time

Euthanasia is the hardest experience you will ever share with the dog. You must therefore avail yourself of the opportunity to prepare for it in the best possible way.

Going to the vet with the dog is probably no problem. To drive back may be tremendously difficult, however — and may even be dangerous. Let somebody else drive you home!

Some prefer to make the trip to the vet alone. They want to have time to gather their thoughts and spend a few last moments with their dog without any interruption. Most prefer to be accompanied by a family member or friend, however.

Many want to get an appointment with the vet as soon as possible after making the decision. They want to get it over with while they are still convinced that they are doing the right thing. It can also be hard to have a certain defined, length of time in front of you.

Others value this last period together especially much. They want to have plenty of time to prepare themselves and plenty of time with the dog. Many have testified to the fact that this final time of togetherness may be the best of all. As rule, it is the physical and mental condition of the dog that will decide how much time is left together.

Picking the Right Place

Euthanasia usually is performed at the vet's or at an animal hospital. Some veterinarians make house calls, if asked.

Some owners prefer to have it done at home, because the dog is in such bad shape that the trip would be too stressful. There is a risk that the dog would become nervous and anxious at a clinic.

When euthanasia is to be carried out in the home, you have to dispose of the body yourself. The veterinarian will not take care of it.

You should avoid euthanasia in the home if you suspect that you will not be strong enough to handle such an emotionally charged situation. Should you faint or break down, the vet will have yet another problem on his hands at a time when he has to devote all his attention to the dog. If the dog is nervous and you are too distraught to be of any help, the situation may turn into a most unpleasant experience.

If you have a dog who, in spite of illness, still wants to protect its territory, it may become even more upset by the vet's intrusion than it would have been being taken to a clinic.

It is important that you weigh these considerations carefully before making a decision. You have to factor in the condition of your pet, its probable reaction to a clinic and a home visit respectively, your own mental state, what to do with the remains etc.

Should you opt for a veterinary clinic, you should try to arrange it so that you do not have to wait. Having to wait among other animal owners who may have young animals with only minor complaints, may be extremely hard.

Methods of Euthanasia

Shooting a dog is neither a very common way of disposing of a companion nor the most humane.

Having a veterinarian perform euthanasia is beyond doubt the most humane way. The vet administers an overdose of anaesthesia which is injected into a vein in one of the front legs. The dog quietly and gently falls asleep. It loses consciousness without experiencing any pain or transition. There is no pain involved, and after a short while the dog is beyond reach.

If the dog is anxious, it may first be given a tranquilizing shot. Some veterinarians do this routinely.

Animals probably do not experience any anxiety before death. They may however feel, and be affected by, our own anxiety and

disquiet before what is taking place. The foremost — and most difficult — duty of a dog owner is therefore to try to be as calm and composed as possible. This is the very best and most loving kind of assistance you can give your dog during its last few hours and minutes in life.

Whether to Be Present

Everybody obviously wants to provide their beloved friend with as calm, loving and dignified end to your time together as possible.

To some, this means cradling their dog in their arms, stroking it and speaking to it reassuringly and lovingly until its very last breath — exactly the same way as they themselves would like to die: in the presence of someone they love.

There is no doubt that the dog feels more secure in the presence of someone it knows well, but it need not necessarily be its owner. Some want to remember their dog as it was, alive and active, and are afraid to disturb this picture of it by assisting at its euthanasia.

Others find it so hard that they cannot take it, so they ask somebody else to be there. This may be wise, if you know that you will not be able to handle the situation. Crying or screaming or desperately trying to interrupt the process, once begun, will not provide the quiet and dignified end that the dog deserves. The veterinarian will obviously find such undisciplined behavior a great strain, one making an already difficult task harder.

A situation like this may turn into an extremely traumatic experience, and you may blame yourselves for years to come for not providing a more dignified end for your dog.

If you think that you can handle the euthanasia, however, it may lead to a sense of peace and harmony. Many find this a last chance to show their dog proof of their affection — a natural way of repaying it for years of friendship and happiness.

Even if the decision to have the dog put away is justified and carefully considered, you may experience a kind of state of shock at the time. This may, paradoxically, be helpful and give you unexpected strength to behave in a calm and dignified fashion and watch your friend fall asleep in your safe and familiar arms.

Watching your pet die in this way is not as terrifying as it may seem. It may leave you with a memory of one of the most beautiful and elevating moments in life.

There is also comfort to be derived from seeing that the dog actually is dead. Then you never have to be haunted by the dreadful suspicion that your dog is being used for painful animal experiments.

If you do not wish to be present at the euthanasia, but still would like to view your pet, the veterinarian will be happy to arrange this.

The way you conclude your relationship with the dog will be very important to the grieving process ahead. Consider the various alternatives at your disposal, and select the one that you will feel the best about. What is done cannot be undone.

Those who are strong enough and loving enough to sit with a dying (patient) in the silence which transcends all words, know that this moment is neither frightening nor painful but the peaceful end to the functioning of the body.

Elisabeth Kübler-Ross

Summary

- Laws against euthanasia protect not only those who are ill, but they also see to it that their next-of-kin is not placed in the difficult situation of having to decide. In the case of an animal owner, this protection does not exist. Responsibility and decision-making are entirely in his hands.

- There is no general advice for those who are facing the difficult decision of whether to have their dog put away. The deciding factor is obviously the dog's quality of life. Does it still retain its happiness and zest for life, or is every day a source of pain?

- The fact that a dog has to take medication or undergo surgery is naturally not the same as that it must be euthanized. Nor is old age sufficient reason, in and of itself.

- The anxiety of certain dogs at the moment of euthanasia may be a reflection of the anxiety of the owner, subconsciously transmitted to the dog. Anxiety before death is probably reserved for us humans alone.

- Being present when a dog is euthanized is not as traumatic as you might think. If you know that you are capable of handling the situation, this experience may lead to a sense of calm and tranquil exaltation.

The Role of the Veterinarian

I was young, I was inexperienced — and in love! That is how Eva characterized herself at the age when she got her first dog. Before Kaj — as the dog was called — was two years old, Eva had had a cruel reminder that life is not always rosy. Not even when you are in love.

She told me her story many years later. At that time her bitterness had subsided, she said, and she had more of a distance to what happened.

This is what she told me:

— Kaj became sick, I didn't realize just how sick, to begin with. But I could see that something was wrong. Although his appetite was enormous and he could have eaten a horse, he just got thinner and thinner. The visits to the vet did not yield any explanation, nor did it result in any change. No one seemed to understand what was wrong with him. I was young and inexperienced and listened politely to the vet's assurances that he would probably get better with time. This is common in young dogs, he said. They have a tremendous appetite, and then they burn off all they consume by being so active. I listened to him, calmed down and allowed myself to be taken in. Kaj did not get better as the vet promised, however, just hungrier and hungrier. Finally, it was clear to everyone that he was wasting away, in the true sense of the word.

I got in touch with another vet, confident that, this time, I was in competent hands. The new veterinarian tackled the case with enormous zest and a decisiveness that made me breathe a sigh of relief. Finally I had found someone who would understand! But he could not figure out what was wrong with Kaj either. Maybe he did not have the resources for a thorough diagnosis and treatment. Kaj was referred to a large animal hospital. The problem was more serious than I had thought.

Then came the day when I had to leave Kaj at the hospital for tests. I was very nervous and anxious and felt terrible at having to leave him. I stood there looking after him as they led him away, praying silently: "Please God, make him well again!" I looked at the veterinarian and directed the same prayer to him — please make him well again. I never spoke out loud — of course the vet would do his very best, regardless of my prayers. I managed to control my worries relatively well, but I left with a lump in my throat.

When I got home I started the most traumatic wait in my life — waiting for the phone to ring. I will actually never forget that phone call. Kaj was seriously ill, as I had suspected. But there is a tremendous difference between suspicion and certainty.

When the phone rang, I felt icy cold. I felt removed from reality. Everything was quiet around me, and I felt lost in space. Some part of my brain managed to take command. I heard myself ask questions, but I no longer remember what I said. The vet answered something, but I don't know what.

I had only one thought — what is best for Kaj? What should I do? Should I let him live or die? Everything revolved around what was the best thing for Kaj.

I thought I heard the vet say that Kaj would never be completely well, and that he would have to be on medication all his life. Actually, it was impossible to tell how long he would live — and whether the medication would be of any help.

One thing was clear — my Kaj would not have to live half a life, just because I wanted his company so badly.

The phone call lasted only a few minutes — and not long after that, Kaj was dead.

When I was talking on the phone, making my decision, I felt curiously distant and removed from what was going on. A few hours later I was beset by regrets, anxiety and questions. What did the vet mean by not completely well and having to be on medication? Was it the same thing as half a life? How long could Kaj have survived with the right treatment — a month, a year, several years?

Today I am older, more confident and, hopefully, more experienced. I would have done things differently today. I am also able to see my reactions more clearly. I was in a state of shock and felt helpless and completely at the mercy of the vet and his words — even though I only caught half of what he said. I wish he had been smarter than I. If he had suspected how I felt, he would have suggested that I wait to make a decision until I had been to see him at the hospital. It was quite far away, that is true, but that would have given me some time to think things over.

I felt very bitter towards that uncaring vet for several years, for so coldly depriving me of the extra time that I needed. Maybe he was as immature and helpless as I?

The Hardest Task of All

The task of a physician and a veterinarian is to cure and save lives, but — in the case of a vet — also to take lives. This is the dark side of a veterinarian's duties. Euthanasia is much more than just a routine act. The attitude and actions of the veterinarian are of enormous importance to the dog owner before, during and after the euthanasia. The owner has usually been in touch with the vet many times, long before the decision concerning euthanasia came up. It is usually the veterinarian who has to deliver the prognosis — thereby setting in motion the process which may ultimately lead to euthanasia.

The vet has to know how to handle emotionally upset and deeply shocked people in an understanding and caring way. In Eva's case, the vet had unfortunately not yet learned this.

No One Remains Unaffected

Those who come into contact with the problems surrounding death cannot help being affected in some way. It may give rise to compassion, anxiety and a feeling of helplessness . . .

To experience, at close hand, the death of another reminds us of the transitory nature of our own life. Seeing others mourn makes us sad and depressed and feeling rather helpless. Their trauma might have been ours. We react differently before feelings like these depending, to some extent, on earlier experiences in life, but also on our personality and on how well we have learnt to handle problems in life.

People, whose profession it is to help and support others in need, must obviously first know themselves and their reactions. If you have a hard time facing your own pain and anxiety and shy away from difficult things like the thought of death, you will obviously find it difficult to be of help to others. The veterinarian frequently finds himself having to confront death and those who mourn.

Even though euthanasia is rather uncomplicated, from a purely technical point of view, it may make an inexperienced veterinarian very much upset. With time, even this part of his job will become more of a routine — a necessary thing if the vet is to be able to survive without psychological damage to himself.

But even vets — like everyone else — react differently to various strong emotions. Some remain more sensitive than others, and find every instance of euthanasia a tremendous strain. If he has known the animal and its owner for many years, the situation will become even more fraught with emotion. Some vets admit, and may show openly, that they are affected. Others strive to maintain a more strict and "professional" attitude.

The latter may be the case when the vet wants to create a calm and secure atmosphere. But it may also have its roots in the insecurity of the vet himself.

Cool Professionalism Versus Compassionate Involvement

Even though it may be important to create a serene and secure atmosphere in which the dog owner feels confidence in the vet, too professional an attitude may have the opposite effect and be mistaken for coldness.

This is a difficult balancing act for the veterinarian who is expected to be both a secure and dependable authority figure and compassionate and emotionally involved at the same time. This can be burdensome, especially to someone who feels affected, but has a hard time showing his feelings.

People expect different things from their vets. Most prefer a compassionate person showing sensitivity and sympathy to someone who only carries out his task correctly and professionally. To a dog owner, euthanasia can never become a routine matter.

Most dog owners stress the importance of support and empathy in their veterinarian. During the period immediately following the death, they often return in their thoughts to the vet to try to find comfort in his words or attitude.

I had come to regard my patients as machinery in need of repair. I then started to listen to the language of my colleagues and their choice of words in a different way. I remember I was giving a lecture at a pediatrics conference that year. Several of my colleagues came in late, explaining that "an interesting case" — a child with threatening diabetic coma — had just been admitted. I realized, with a shock, what a distance this attitude was creating between the physicians and their "case" — which happened to be a very sick and frightened child with anxious parents.

I saw clearly that I myself — even though I had tried to resist it — also used this defense mechanism against pain and failure. It hurt, so I withdrew just as the patients needed me more than ever . . .

I used to think that it was necessary to keep a certain distance, but most doctors carry it to an extreme, in my opinion. . . .

The cool, professional care that we are taught is unrealistic. Instead, we need to learn a reasonable care which allows us to show our emotions without reducing our capacity for making decisions.

Bernie S. Siegel

In an article published in *Hundsport*, a veterinarian described his first case of euthanasia in the following way:

"She arrived at the clinic with her dog at the appointed time. She wanted to hold it herself, and seemed very calm and collected at the time. I inserted the needle, gave the injection and told her that it was finally over. She then started to cry violently, cradling the dog and throwing her arms around my neck, embracing me in her despair and search for comfort. Inexperienced as I was, and shocked at her sudden outburst of emotion, I was at a loss for words. Then I too, was seized by the gravity of it all and burst into tears. It was, if I remember correctly, in some way liberating, standing there with our arms around each other. At least, I hope in retrospect that she knew that I empathized with her great grief."

Greater sympathy and compassion than that is hard to imagine. I am sure that this dog owner remembers her veterinarian with great fondness and gratitude. Even if all vets are not able to show such empathy, he or she remains the one immediately at hand when someone who has just lost her pet is in special need of support and comfort.

Distancing and Aggressiveness

Not all dog owners react with the same spontaneity as this woman. Some withdraw completely and become inaccessible. Some pretend to be totally unaffected and reject everyone. In such cases, tact, courage and insight into human nature are called for on the part of the veterinarian, who is faced with a fellow human being who is in dire need of contact and sympathy but who is afraid to show his or her feelings openly and instead does everything to hide them. This attitude obviously makes the vet guarded, since the whole body language of the owner seems to say:

"Leave me alone, I can manage on my own. I don't want your help or comfort."

A quick caress on the cheek, a light pat on the back or the shoulder may be all that is needed to loosen up and release pent-up emotions. And no one has to lose face.

We have mistakenly been taught to leave people alone when things are difficult. On the contrary, that is when most of us have a real need of human contact and compassion — even though we may not dare to admit it or even less ask for it.

To keep aggressiveness and unfounded accusations in their proper perspective is difficult for all of us, including harried veterinarians. It takes patience and understanding not to get locked in a defense position or maybe even counterattack. Usually these outbursts are dramatic but short-lived and soon turn into silence or a flood of tears. Of course the veterinarian may resent being the target for outbursts of this kind — and, at the same time, be expected to show compassion. Maybe it will be easier if he keeps in mind that he is confronted with an unbalanced person and whose need for consolation and help is acute.

The Veterinarian as Guide

It may take weeks or even months for the dog owner to arrive at a carefully considered decision about euthanasia. The same questions keep arising, over and over. To most dog owners, this is a serious and, in most cases, completely necessary process — a kind of preparatory anxiety which later makes it easier to handle grief in a rational way.

Many vets are aware of the importance of allowing the dog owner to make their own decision as to whether or when the dog is to be put away. The task of the veterinarian is to provide factual information concerning the state of the dog and its possibilities for recovery. No matter how justified the vet's advice may be, it may be mistaken for a lack of understanding and respect for the owner's feelings. If the vet suggests that the dog be euthanized, it may have exactly the opposite effect. The owner may become disappointed or aggressive and may, in fact, tune out all factual information in the future. At worst, the owner may avoid all veterinarians, thereby possibly prolonging the suffering of his animal. Alternatively, the owner may follow the advice of the vet, then change his mind and vent all his bitterness and spite on him.

It is important to the peace of mind of the owner to know that he has considered all the implications of his decision. If the dog is not in pain, and if its condition permits a certain grace period, it is the duty of every veterinarian to help arrive at a carefully considered decision that has not been made under pressure.

Trying to protect the feelings of the owner by partial truths or by an overly optimistic assessment may have the same adverse effects. Grown-ups do not want to be treated like children — nor do children! Honest and forthright behavior and clear and understandable information about the dog's condition is always appreciated. This will provide the best foundation for a carefully considered decision no matter how difficult the case.

The grieving process which has already begun is usually intensified at the arrival at the clinic or right after the death of the dog. In showing understanding for the grief of the owner, the veterinarian may help ease his or her sorrow. If he takes it upon himself to explain in detail what has happened and what is about to happen, the owner will not have to ask questions. This will also remove any thoughts and suspicions that the dog will actually not be put to sleep or that the euthanasia will not be carried out in a humane and painless way.

The owner may imagine that the dog will not be put away, but will be used for medical research. It may ease the worries of the owner considerably if this is categorically denied.

Shock and Guilt Feelings

The owner is usually in a state of shock when he is first told of the seriousness of the dog's condition and when the euthanasia is carried out. Much of what the veterinarian says then is therefore poorly assimilated. Sometimes the owner has to call the veterinarian repeatedly to receive the same information and answers over and over.

These consultations are a necessary form of reassurance. There are unfortunately those who are afraid to avail themselves of this option for fear of wasting the vet's time.

Children are more prone than adults to make a mystery out of the dog's death and to think that they themselves have somehow caused its death. In moments of anger at something the dog did or did not do or in a fit of jealousy over attention, the child may have expressed a wish to see it dead. When the dog then actually dies, the child may think that he or she caused it.

Children may also imagine that it is some form of punishment for something they said or did not do. They are, as we all know, not always nice to animals. When the dog dies, children may remember occasions when they did not treat the dog particularly well. Reproach like this may haunt a child for a long time. Sometimes the child may be afraid to tell anybody of its fears, terrified as he is at having done something wrong.

The vet is often better equipped than the parents to tell a child why his or her pal has to die. A talk like this may do more than just rid the child of painful fantasies and guilt feelings. It also conveys the message that the child is important and respected. If you treat a child right, you will often find that he or she is better able to handle truth than many grown-ups.

One of the most important tasks of a veterinarian is thus to provide thorough information. How this is done is also important.

By not limiting himself to diagnosing and naming the disease but by also describing the symptoms of the illness in understandable terms, a vet may remove causes of anxiety by explaining what medication, continued treatment or an operation might do for the sick animal.

The dog owner usually blames himself for faults or omissions. Self-reproach and guilt are central themes in every grieving process. By dispensing factual and understandable information, a veterinarian may ease the guilt feelings of the owner and be of great comfort.

The same is true when an animal has died or been killed suddenly and unexpectedly before you have had time to get in touch with a vet. Even if the vet is never able to remove the entire burden of guilt, it may help to be told by an authority figure what you actually already know yourself, namely that we have no control over circumstances, and that it could have happened to anyone, no matter how careful.

It sometimes happens, in the case of an accident or acute illness, that the dog will die on its way to the clinic or soon after arrival. Here too, the vet may find himself confronted with a deeply shaken person who may be unable or unwilling to acknowledge that the dog is dead, regardless of what the veterinarian tells them. The trauma may be enormous. Accusations and appeals to the vet to do something alternate. From a strictly practical point of view, there is obviously no point in intervening once the dog is beyond all help. Some form of "rescue attempt" can occasionally be of great psychological value to the owner anyway, since he may believe — even under less stressful circumstances — that the vet would not consider a seriously ill or hurt animal worth saving. Veterinary intervention may therefore be valuable also in this case. It will leave the dog owner with the feeling that the veterinarian really did everything in his or her power.

Afterwards ...

Once the dog has been euthanized and cremated or the body has been returned to the owner, the responsibility of the vet ceases.

There are vets who make it a practice to keep in touch with the owner for some time following the death of the dog. This form of contact, whether by letter or by phone, may be very important to the bereaved. Many continue to have a need to have their decision confirmed, and to hear that the dog would not have gotten better and that they did everything in their power.

Never underestimate the value of this kind of reassurance. The owner's thoughts continue to revolve around the dog long after it is gone. Many would therefore welcome a talk with their veterinarian after the first grief and shock have subsided, but are afraid to bother him with further questions.

A call or a letter from the vet will never come as an unpleasant reminder of something you would prefer to forget, but is rather a sign that somebody cares, that somebody you respect understands and accepts your grief.

Guilt and blame are, as I said, a central theme in the grieving process. Even though you cannot expect the vet to have the competence to assume the role of professional therapist — or that he should want to do so — he or she can make the grief work of the owner easier by just such a sign of empathy.

It may turn out that the owner is having an abnormally hard time emerging from his grief. If it has not abated since the animal died, the veterinarian could recommend that the bereaved seek professional help. People react very differently to such a suggestion. It is therefore important to stress that "prolonged" grief is not a sign of "mental illness." The problem may have its roots in a number of causes such as earlier experiences, the circumstances surrounding the death, the strength of the attachment, etc.

Many — even those who are mourning a beloved animal — receive the suggestion that there is help to be had with a liberating sense of relief.

Wrongful Treatment?

It goes without saying that a veterinarian is capable of misjudgements and mistakes, just like anyone else. At worst, his mistake or wrongful treatment can lead to the death or incapacitation of the patient.

Should this be the case, the owner will understandably be bitter and aggressive and look for a scapegoat — in this case the veterinarian.

If you actually suspect that your vet is guilty of wrongful treatment or has misjudged your pet's condition, you should obviously raise the matter personally with him or her. If you remain unsatisfied, you should contact his superior if there is one. You can also turn to another veterinarian or to his professional organization.

None of this will give you your dog back or ease your grief. Nevertheless, it is of utmost importance that the matter be resolved — for all parties concerned. If a veterinarian is guilty of one or several obvious mistakes it will naturally have to be brought to the attention of those in authority.

Mental Assessment at Veterinary Clinics

An ordinary dog owner is obviously not capable of assessing the professional competence of a vet.

An expert within a given field is often expected to possess far-reaching knowledge outside his own specialty. This means that veterinarians often find themselves facing questions that lie outside their area of competence.

This is especially true about psychological counseling, for example assessing the mental state of a dog. Many mistakenly think that this lies within a veterinarian's field of competence.

A vet has a medical degree. He is familiar with the physiology of animals, how to prevent and cure physical illnesses, how to ease pain, what physical treatment should be prescribed etc. He is seldom competent to assess or treat a mental condition, however. It is important to bear this in mind, especially since there is a variety of opinions within this field.

It is just as unrealistic to expect a vet to provide professional help and information about the mental condition of a dog as it is to ask a surgeon to cure fear of darkness, lack of self-confidence, phobias etc. Most vets are aware of the limits of their competence, and do not pretend to be experts on anything else. If need be, their patients will be referred to trained experts for psychological treatment.

Never ask your vet to assess the mental condition of your dog. If this happens anyway and results in the euthanasia of your dog, you may blame both the veterinarian and yourself for years to come.

Summary

- The vet has a central role to play before, during and after euthanasia.

- The words of the vet are often the only thing the dog owner has to go by, the only thing he or she has to rely on.

- One of the most important functions of a veterinarian is to provide factual information on the dog's condition. How this is done is obviously important if the owner is to make a well-informed decision in peace and quiet.

- Body contact, in the form of a light touch, may release pent-up feelings.

- The veterinarian can be of great help in the grieving process. Not least by easing any feelings of guilt.

Managing Your Grief

Berith is a strong woman, self-assured, successful in her profession, active and full of initiative. She is the kind of person who usually succeeds in her undertakings and who gives rise both to envy and admiration. She has always been a steadfast friend and counselor. If you have a problem or need to talk to someone, Berith is always there.

But one time Berith was not her usual self. She felt helpless and indecisive, was unable to make decisions, and became irritable and would burst into tears over trifling matters if things did not go right. This was after she had lost her dog.

She contacted me four months after her dog died, and we became friends. In the beginning, she was shocked at her own transformation.

— It is as if I no longer know myself, she said. I, who have always been strong and competent, will soon be unable to decide even what to wear. Whenever I am confronted with a choice, no matter how trivial, I am unable to make up my mind. I am totally confused, then I give up and start to cry. My friends no longer recognize me. They have actually started to avoid me, and my husband has had it up to here with my tears and tantrums. But the worst thing is my grief. I can't stop thinking of Bimbo. Everyday, something reminds me of him and it hurts. I cry almost every day, and when I don't cry I am mostly angry. I don't know how to handle my grief. I am at my wit's end, and there is no one to talk to. I feel that my friends are tired of me, even if no one says so outright. They are probably every bit as surprised as I am at my transformation. I do try to act normal, but I can't. Either I am depressed and feel that life is over, or else I am mad at myself and at the fact that no one seems to understand. In between, I am exhausted and just want to sleep.

Our talks finally made it clear what had happened. Berith had tried to end and suppress her grief too soon. She — and her acquaintances — considered her strong enough to handle her grief without too many problems. However, she had a strong personality and was full of energy. She was a person of powerful feelings, and she had loved her dog intensively. What she never realized is that if your devotion is strong, your grief will also be intense.

Berith was conducting a needless and unfair war on herself in trying to live up to her own expectations and to those of her surroundings. It was a great relief to be able to view her grief from a different perspective. She stopped worrying about having changed and allowed herself to be seen in all her grief.

— More than two years have passed, and I see clearly how I have changed, she says. I am not the same, but I don't view my transformation as something negative. Thank God, I recovered my ability to act and to make decisions. But deep inside I am probably a little less certain — of myself, of life, and of everything around. Maybe I am also a bit more humble. I see this as a wonderful legacy of my darling Bimbo.

Even when the preconditions for a constructive and normal grieving process appear to be the very best, as in the case of Berith, grief is never something to be treated lightly. Nor are there any shortcuts or simple ways to escape the pain which inevitably accompanies the loss of a loved one. But grief may be handled more or less constructively. Our insight into grief, into ourselves and our own reactions will ultimately be decisive.

What Has Your Dog Been to You?

Many answer that question by referring to exercise or company. And there is no doubt that those are two reasons why people keep dogs. But it tells us nothing about why most of us form such a strong attachment to our dog.

While your dog is still alive, you should give some thought to what your dog actually means to you, and what needs are satisfied by it. This kind of analysis and insight may be very important later, when it comes to understanding and accepting grief.

To many, a dog is a close friend, someone who provides comfort and whom you can trust. But the dog may have a deeper significance. It may represent the brother or the sister you always longed for but never had. Maybe it has become the only trustworthy and reliable friend in a life marked by repeated disappointments in human relationships.

In many instances, the dog serves as an important link to other people, sometimes even the salvation from a life of total isolation and loneliness. In such cases, the sense of grief and bereavement will obviously be very intense.

If you have given some thought to what your dog actually means to you, you will have made it easier to understand and accept your grief when it strikes. It will be easier to be gentle on yourself, to let yourself mourn properly, rather than trying to brush your grief aside with the aid of artificial subterfuges and excuses.

Since a dog fulfills several needs, it leaves behind more than one void. A multitude of previously meaningful routines and activities also come to a halt. Being out in nature, having someone to care for and pay attention to, someone to stroke and pet — the more little things like these that you lose, the worse you will feel.

This is probably the main reason why many dog owners acquire a new dog within a short period of time. Sometimes it works out very well. To a certain extent, the new dog does replace the old one. But sometimes it does not work. You don't have the strength to devote yourself to someone new while your heart is still breaking from mourning the loss of the loved one. Therefore, many prefer to wait. Others realize that they don't want another dog, for a variety of reasons. To them, it is more important to understand what the dog meant to them, so that they are able to find meaningful alternatives.

Accepting Grief

The first step in a constructive grieving process is accepting your grief and expressing it. There are those who try to escape their grief by filling their time with intensive work or a multitude of activities. This may provide a certain temporary relief.

We humans react differently to grief. We all have to handle our individual grief in whatever way is right for us. A change of scenery may provide some relief. But it may be hard to make the decision to go away. A vacation, which may be tempting under normal circumstances, may lose its allure completely when we are weighed down with grief. After some time has been allowed to pass, a trip, may however, may turn out to be a much needed and stimulating

---

I had planted some twenty trees. In the beginning, they grew surprisingly rapidly. But then we had a snow storm that coated each branch and twig with a layer of snow and ice. Instead of yielding gracefully to the burden, the trees proudly resisted and broke. I had to cut them down, for they had not learned the wisdom of spruces and firs which know to yield to the inevitable and bend their branches. So they survive . . .

And what happens if we try to resist the blows in life rather than absorb them? What happens if we refuse to bend like the reed and instead offer resistance like an oak tree? It is simple. We set into motion a number of inner conflicts and become restless, forced, nervous and neurotic. If we go one step further, closing our eyes to reality altogether and withdraw within a shell, we will sooner or later go mad.

Dale Carnegie

---

nudge back to life. The most intense grieving period will then be over, and we will have begun to adjust to our loss and loneliness.

All our memories will obviously still be there and will probably intensify as we return home. But by then, we will have hopefully gathered new strength with which to face any waiting challenges.

If you cry easily, and feel the need to do so, let no one — not even you yourself — try to prevent you from expressing your grief in this way. If the liberating tears do not come easily to you, and you prefer to sit quietly by yourself, you should demand that right from your surroundings.

If you feel the need to talk about your dog and about the past, you should seek out people who would understand or at least would be willing to listen. Explain to them that you are not asking for their help. No one can take on somebody else's pain, but there is often a need for a sympathetic ear. Talking is one way of working on your grief.

The next step in the grieving process is probably the hardest: accepting the loss. My dog is gone forever. It does not matter what I do or what I think. Recognizing this fact is usually incredibly difficult.

We try to resist in various ways; one is by living in the past. Even if it is OK to live with your memories and to think about what has happened, to ask, wonder etc., the day inevitably comes when you have to face and accept reality as it is. This is necessary in order to break out of your grief and gradually return to life.

Feelings of panic and anxiety may be more common than we think, but they seldom lead to a nervous breakdown. If you accept and understand these feelings, they will eventually go away. If your feelings of panic and anxiety are strong enough to cause concern, you should seek professional help. Sometimes it will require only a few, or even a single, visit to a therapist.

Settling Your Guilt

Settle any feelings of guilt you may have. Whether justified or not, it is important that these feelings not be neglected or ignored. Instead, look at them realistically. You may choose to talk to a friend about why you are blaming yourself. When you talk openly about such feelings they assume their right proportions. Maybe you were unduly

severe with your dog on some occasion or punished it unnecessarily hard. Maybe you were negligent, or feel that you should have acted differently.

If your feelings of guilt are warranted, it is of vital importance that you sort them out. Thoughts and emotions that are so painful that you want to suppress them have a tendency to turn to obsession if you don't subject them to close scrutiny.

No matter how great or small our guilt, we must accept our own insufficiency. We all make mistakes, and no one is master of all the circumstances in life. Not until we finally face our guilt feelings are we able to accept and forgive this. Not until then are we able to leave them behind.

Finally, let yourself grieve — on your own terms. If you want to bury your dog or arrange some other ritual, go ahead! Don't let anyone dissuade you or make fun of you. Accept grief for what it is, a painful part of life for those who are courageous enough to love.

Burial

If the euthanasia takes place at home, you will have to plan beforehand what is to happen with the remains. If it takes place at a clinic or in an animal hospital, on the other hand, disposal of the body will usually be taken care of. If this service is lacking, the remains will revert to the owner who then is charged with final disposal.

We humans react very differently. Some do not want the memory of their friend permanently associated with a certain burial site. To others, handing over their pet without some form of leavetaking or burial ceremony is unthinkable.

Many derive a certain peace of mind from the burial act. The burial will give you additional time and will provide a gentler transition to a life without your dog. The burial is perceived as the irrevocable end of a loving relationship.

You have to make sure that there are no regulations to keep you from burying the dog in the place you select. In built-up areas, burial may only take place in official pet cemeteries. These exist in most large cities.

Regulations, costs and customs vary. Certain cemeteries only offer ground burial, others only a place for the ashes of cremated animals. Others offer both these options. There may also be private burial grounds.

There may be restrictions concerning grave decorations. You should check the terms governing rental of the plot. The regulations governing your municipality are available through the court house.

There is every reason to give some thought — while the dog is still alive — to whether you want to have it buried when the day comes. Then you do not have to think about it later, when you will probably be in a state of shock.

It is important that you consider carefully beforehand what you want to do. Don't let the decision be based on the reactions of others. Your grief belongs to you. How you manage it, and how you want to your relationship with your beloved dog to end is your business and your decision.

Concluding the Grieving Process

Putting an end to your grief at a certain point and deciding that the time for grieving is now over is every bit as important as accepting and expressing your loss and allowing yourself enough time to grieve.

At first glance, such a statement may seem totally absurd. Is it possible to consciously decide to start or stop the grieving process?

Grief is something you experience, something you cannot avoid, no matter how much you would want to. But grief is also affected by our own grief-enhancing thoughts. Our way of thinking does affect our emotions and the forms our grief take.

Immediately following the loss of a dear friend it is hard, not to say impossible, to avoid thinking about what has happened.

Every day may be a painful reminder of your loss. But as time goes on, you think about it less and less often. Your grief is no longer an abyss. Your thoughts start to move in other directions.

You keep returning to the positive things and realize that you are getting along quite well, after all. This gradual process is automatic. Remaining sad and depressed for ever is simply too draining.

Crises — Blessings in Disguise?

Our own thoughts are able to affect the grieving process positively or negatively. We are not just "at the mercy" of our feelings. Emotions can, to a certain extent, be guided and controlled.

When we lose someone close, existence seems unfair and meaningless. Our life changes, and important everyday routines come to a halt. We have every right to be sad. But being sad is not entirely bad, and nor is mourning. Much strength is, oddly enough, to be derived from sorrow. Black despair forces us to face ourselves, maybe for the first time. This is frightening at first, because we are not used to penetrating this far into our own minds. Crises are the ultimate tests in life, if we do not shy away from them. Far from making us more fragmented, they make us more complete and stronger human beings.

We watch sad movies, crying at the misfortunes of the main characters. We read books about unrequited love, we listen to songs of lost happiness. We repeatedly expose ourselves to similar emotional upheaval — and pay money for the privilege. But this "pain" is not our own. These stories may induce strong emotions, but we forget them quite readily when we return to reality.

But when grief pays a visit to our home, it becomes concrete and real and can no longer be ignored. We are trapped in the midst of our sorrow, unable to escape. We are affected in a completely different way. This grief belongs to us.

But grief is not only anxiety and despair. In its midst are beautiful memories which we tend gently and lovingly.

Do Not Reinforce Your Grief

Below you will find listed some examples of grief-enhancing and destructive thoughts:

- This is the worst thing that has ever happened to me. It is unfair, terrible and disastrous, and I don't think I will ever get over it.

- Life is terribly unfair. Why should this happen to me?

- I am the most miserable and the loneliest human being in the world. No one understands what it is like and how I feel.

- Life is totally meaningless. Nothing will ever be the same.

- Nothing will ever complement or fulfill my life in the same way as my darling dog.

- Just think how many mistakes I made while my dog was alive. It is awful. I will never forgive myself for being such a bad person — I guess I still am.

No one would have to be miserable and unhappy if he truly knew himself. Deepened self-awareness runs like a thread through the labyrinth of our experiences leading to greater clarity and simplicity . . .

We have no reason to lose hope. There is a way out of even the most difficult situations and the most painful experiences. We seldom see it, because it is surprisingly close at hand. It is simply to turn around and immerse ourselves in the clear and calm waters of our innermost being.

Paul Brunton

Thoughts like these are destructive and harmful, but are far from uncommon — and are not always caused by grief.

All you have to do is to repeat thoughts like these a few times every day, and you will find yourself in a miserable state of negative feelings and depression. Negative thought patterns are extremely common. We are unfortunately usually unaware that we are reinforcing and prolonging our pain and grief in this way. Our thoughts are governed by habits, constructive or destructive. We resist with every fibre in our body when called on to change our negative thought patterns. This is especially true of old and well-established thought habits.

A Positive Dialogue

All our experiences are enacted and relived in our thoughts and in our conscious. You should therefore pay careful attention to your thoughts and what you are telling yourself. Try to escape the notion that you are a victim. Try to think positively.

This is easy to say but hard to do. It is easy to keep falling back into old established thought patterns. As soon as you find that you have made such a "mistake," you should quickly add a positive footnote or start a dialogue with yourself in order to turn to a more positive ways of thinking:

- It is true that things are difficult today and that I miss my dog terribly, but why shouldn't I be able to cope with this situation? I have encountered problems and difficulties before in life, and I have managed. Like when . . . and the time when . . . and the time when . . . !

- Who ever said that life was fair, or that I should walk unscathed through life, unlike everybody else? What happened happened. There is nothing to do but to accept that.

- I feel unhappy right now, but am I actually as lonely and deserted as all that? Isn't there a single person who would understand how I feel? This person, for instance, or that person, or. . . . I'll call. . . .

- It will never be the same, that's true. But changes can be meaningful and character-building. There are still a lot of things, for instance. . . .

- No one can ever replace my darling dog. But there may be another who will enrich my life in a different and maybe equally rewarding way.

- Of course I was wrong and made mistakes, but don't we all? I did stupid things because I didn't know any better, or didn't think, or was in a bad mood. Actually, how many mistakes did I make compared with things that were good? Like when. . . . and when. . . . Actually, I am no worse than anyone else.

It is possible to turn self-reproach and other negative thoughts into something positive which builds a feeling of confidence and hope. But remember that it takes repeated efforts. It is too easy to fall back on the conviction that you are at the mercy of your feelings.

A wise man said that the important thing is not what happens to us, but how we respond to the situations that we encounter in life.

The Healing Power of Nature

Maybe you have a hard time putting up with those around you, or even with yourself. In such cases, nature has proved to be a wonderful source of healing and renewal. Listen to the birds or the rustling of the wind in the leaves. Enjoy a colorful sunset — or why not the sight of a cat stalking a butterfly.

Every life, every season, every change in nature has a beauty of its own. It does not go away, unless we decide to bar it from our lives. At first, beauty may hurt, as may life itself. You have just been deprived of the most beautiful thing in life — loving somebody else. Let nature and the life around you and your own positive thoughts bring back wonderful memories as a balm against sorrow and dark thoughts.

Prolonged Grief

The grieving process may last for a year or more. During this period, your grief will vary in intensity and strength from deep and dark despair to calmer and more accepting phases.

The first few days and weeks are obviously the hardest. As weeks and months go by, your grief will become less intense and easier to handle. It may return from time to time with renewed vigor, however, and may make itself felt even after several years.

This is normal for a grieving process. The memory of the one you have lost stays with you — and this is something we want to live with, cultivate and keep. It no longer causes the same pain as before.

But sometimes the grieving process is interrupted. You can get

---

Positive and negative thoughts cannot occupy the mind simultaneously. It is your duty to see to it that it is the positive thoughts that keep your mind busy. This is where habits are helpful. Make it a habit always to have positive thoughts!

Napoleon Hill

---

stuck and find yourself unable to move forward. There are various explanations why grief work may be prolonged. Quite often unresolved guilt feelings are involved.

It is also quite common that you think that you ought to go continue to grieve for a while longer. You may not wish your grief to appear too superficial. Or you may feel that you owe it to yourself and to the dead pet to grieve longer than you actually need to. People quite often wait to get a new dog because it would feel like an act of betrayal to the old one.

The idea that you ought to grieve longer than you actually do is almost as common as the feeling that you are not allowed to grieve as long as you would like. In both cases, it may result in an exacerbated and prolonged grief process because you have not been able to work through your grief and loss in a constructive way.

Prolonged grief may also have its roots in a feeling that you wants to show your surroundings — over and over — that you actually are grieving! Some do everything within their power to hide their grief, for fear of the reactions of the world around them. The less understanding a grieving person receives, the more desperate the need to repress his or her grief. Now you are trapped in a vicious circle. Your grief is prolonged because you are constantly trying to prove a point. If and when acceptance finally comes, you breathe a sigh of relief: "My friends have realized that my dog was worth mourning." Finally you are free to forget about grief.

No matter what the reasons for the extended grieving process, it is of vital importance — and maybe even necessary — that you seek professional help.

One of the most important reasons for concluding the grieving process is that grief constitutes a strain and danger to your health. Any acute crisis always entails a state of enormous stress, accompanied by various physical and psychological symptoms. Grief weakens you temporarily. Your immune defenses are lowered. Whenever your appetite for life or zest is low, you find yourself at risk for various illnesses. If your grief is prolonged, you will remain at risk longer than necessary.

You used to hear it said that "she died from grief" or "she died from a broken heart." Today we don't put it that way, but our psychological state is sooner or later clearly reflected in our physical state of health. There is consequently every reason in the world to try to get back to normal after an intensive period of grief.

Are there any guidelines about how long the grieving process may take?

Your grief should have abated somewhat after three to six months, or at least be a few shades lighter. If it remains as intense after this length of time, it means that you are stuck for some reason, and have failed to cross an invisible barrier.

Old and unmanaged grief takes longer to cure than a tragedy in the recent past, because the latter is more real to you.

Do not hesitate to seek the help you need!

Summary

- If you analyze exactly what your dog means to you, it will be easier to comprehend and accept your grief when the blow comes. It will also be easier to be easy on yourself, to allow yourself to grieve instead of rejecting grief.

- The first step in all constructive grief work is to express your grief.

- It is more important than you think to settle your feelings of guilt. Whether called for or not, these feelings must be examined and acknowledged. If you try to avoid them, they may fester in your mind with unforeseeable consequences.

- It is just as important to find your way out of your grief as it is to learn to accept it. To put an end to it and start thinking in positive terms may be difficult, but it is nevertheless absolutely necessary.

- The grieving process may be disturbed or exacerbated for some reason. The bereaved person may get stuck, unable to proceed. In this case, professional help is helpful — and may even be necessary.

Helping Others

I was on a trip to Japan when I received a call one day from my closest friend in Gothenburg. Her dog had just died. Since we had earlier talked about how hard it would be when that happened, it felt natural for Lisa to call. I had known her dog Valle for many years and knew that they were very attached to each other. I now had occasion to share her grief. It felt difficult to be so far away. Her letter increased my worries. I could read between the lines that she was floundering. It was clear that Lisa was in the midst of a very difficult period in life.

Right after the death of her dog, Lisa encountered an unexpected amount of sympathy and understanding. She learned eventually that it was her husband who was behind it. He functioned as a kind of safety net, simply "ordering" their friends not to act as if nothing had happened. Everybody participated openly in her sorrow. Some sent flowers and condolence cards. Lisa was shown more sympathy and understanding than most others in the same situation.

Time passed, and Lisa's tragedy was soon a thing of the past. For two months she lived as if in a daze of confusion. Everybody now expected her to go back to normal. Lisa did emerge from her state of shock, true, but experienced only emptiness and a sense of loss. She realized to her horror that everyone now expected her grief to be over. She reacted by suppressing her emotions.

Two months later I was back home, and we saw each other again. I could see right away that Lisa had changed. Was there anything I could do for her that nobody else had been able to do? Maybe. I was not afraid of her sorrow or her tears. I knew that her grieving process was neither strange nor abnormal or something that had to be suppressed at all cost.

It is now six months since Valle died. Lisa and I laugh sometimes, and sometimes we cry. Six months is not a long time, but it can be an eternity to those who have lost a dear friend.

Lisa and I still talk a lot about the past. We talk about death, about grief, about life and love. We try to understand — and sometimes we succeed. In a way we are sharing a burden, but one which can never be as heavy to me. Lisa's grief belongs to her. I just try, as much as I can, to make her life a little easier. Not necessarily by making her laugh or forget, but mostly by being there and by listening. I share her musings, her worries and her thoughts. It is not at all difficult, and I don't do it with a heavy heart. On the contrary, our friendship makes it easy for me — a friendship which furthermore has become stronger and deeper during this period.

Nothing is actually easier than being supportive of someone you love. It hurts to witness grief and suffering, but shying away from it is worse. By keeping the bereaved company on the way, we lighten more than grief. We are obeying the most important and most beautiful commandment of all — that of love. And in our hearts we know that we are doing the right thing.

"Hope All Goes Well"

Our very language shows how unaccustomed we are to coming face to face with the grief and suffering of others.

What should we say? Words are insufficient or unsuitable. You can hardly say "hope all goes well" to a friend who is having her dog put away the following day! Nor is "things will work out" especially good. "I am sorry" or "I understand" may also feel inadequate and paltry.

There we are, lacking the right words and overwhelmed by a feeling of helplessness. It is not surprising that so many opt for saying nothing at all, or pretend as if nothing had happened. And yet, so little is needed to brighten things a bit. Just because we are not afraid to meet raw grief head on it does not necessarily follow that we are expected to be able to lighten or eliminate it.

Expert or Fellow Human?

There are those who think that grief is nothing to worry about or pay attention to. People have grieved since the beginning of time, and have had to get along without the help of experts and psychological insight. Why should we complicate things all of a sudden? And many do manage to handle their grief in such a way that they quickly recover, and seemingly without too much difficulty.

Expressions of grief and loss have changed, as have the rituals surrounding death. It is more difficult than it used to be to grieve naturally. Sorrow and loss are no longer taken for granted in today's society. To many, it is therefore important to learn to mourn, though it may sound strange, and to learn the meaning of grief.

Then there is the view that grief is not a thing for us laymen to meddle in or try to help others get over. Those who are struggling with their grief should seek experienced professional help instead. Friends and relatives are better off remaining passive, in order not to make the situation worse.

Easing someone's grief is obviously something every compassionate person can do. All that is needed is understanding, listening, being there, and expressing your sympathy. You don't have to be a therapist to do that.

When we come across someone who has lost a close friend — whether a person or an animal — all that is needed is to become somewhat more emotionally engaged than usual. Maybe it is this that frightens us so that we prefer to withdraw and turn it over to experts. An understanding friend is often of greater help than certified professionals, be they psychologists, veterinarians, doctors or ministers.

It goes without saying that there are instances when professional help becomes necessary. This is especially true when long periods of time have gone by without the bereaved getting over his feelings of grief and guilt. It is not the intensity of his grief, but rather its duration, that calls for expert intervention. You may be able to make a contribution, as a fellow human being, by persuading the bereaved to seek the help of a therapist.

Misguided Consideration

Since an important part of the grieving process consists of talking about what has taken place, it almost always feels like a betrayal or rebuff if the people around you pretend that nothing has happened. Nor is it good to address the bereaved in an exaggeratedly cheerful and upbeat fashion or to try to change him by exhortations and advice. Saying "things will work out, you know" has its roots in your own insecurity, and probably has the opposite effect from the one intended.

What should we do then to avoid appearing clumsy or intrusive? You would like to be tactful and non-interfering. But to "interfere" may sometimes be the same thing as caring!

Nor does it work to avoid the painful topic in order not to remind someone unnecessarily of his grief. How can you remind someone of something that fills his thoughts night and day? Such "considerate" behavior is easily misinterpreted and may be taken as a sign of lack of interest rather than consideration.

Your help may sometimes be rejected — it is a risk you have to take. This may be the reason why so many opt for not doing anything at all and just stay away.

Those who grieve do not have the strength just then. That is something you have to respect and accept without feeling hurt. Even so, they got the message and will not forget that you got in touch and that you cared. If you are not afraid to try again, you will eventually bring some light into their darkness — though you may not realize it at the time. You have shown that they are worth your sympathy, and that you accept and share their sorrow. Life may, after all, be worth living.

If you are afraid to express your sympathy, it may be a sign of your own anxiety. We often run away from difficult and painful experiences. Witnessing heart-rending grief and not knowing how to ease it is possibly the hardest thing of all.

Just remember that the need of those who grieve is neither for grand gestures nor complicated phrases. Just for a friendly, attentive and sympathetic listener.

Learning to Listen

There are some who possess a well-developed, almost exaggerated need to help others, even to the point of trying to shoulder their burdens. When someone like that comes across a bereaved in desperate need of someone who will listen, he or she seldom remains satisfied just being available. A latent caring need is awakened, often coupled with a deep desire for a grand gesture to ease the pain of the bereaved. As a result, he may go too far both, in word and in deed. He desperately wants to say or do something of decisive help, and in his eagerness may not realize that he is speaking to deaf ears.

Instead, you might start by talking about what has happened in a calm and confident way. Saying "I heard what happened and I am really sorry" might become the opening of a valuable dialogue for both parties. There may not be much said, but the bereaved has been given the message: I care and I am here if you need me.

No past exists to a person who is grieving deeply. It hurts too much to think of the past. Nor is there any future, only a painful present that has to be endured, a minute, an hour, a day at a time. Here, a helping hand is needed, someone to say: I am here, and I won't let you drown in grief and pain.

There is no excuse for not coming to the rescue or letting someone you like waste away before your unseeing and unsympathetic eyes. To lose someone you love is truly to die a little. To lose your friends in addition may, at its worst, lead to slow emotional atrophy. Grief is as deep and traumatic as the mourner experiences it. Sorrow can never be judged or estimated from the outside.

If you really want to be available and help, it is therefore not enough to send a card or some flowers — even if this obviously is better than nothing at all.

Nor does a phone call and a "get in touch when you feel better" do much good, for a grieving person very seldom gets in touch. He or she simply does not have the strength. Therefore you have to keep reminding them that you are there, even though you may be rebuffed.

Don't ever worry about disturbing someone in his or her grief. Don't think that the bereaved wants to be left alone. There is more than enough loneliness — endless nights when you are alone with your agony.

There are even those who, out of kindness, have rushed out to buy a new dog as a surprise for a close friend or a child whose dog has died. In such a situation, the mourner is obviously ill prepared to welcome a new animal. Even if the gesture is thoughtful and well-intended at heart, it may complicate the life both for the bereaved and for the new dog who is neither wanted nor welcome.

Since pain is unavoidable, those who want to help must be prepared to share the pain, to regard it as a token of friendship . . .

Help is thus transmitted through silent communication and devoted understanding. It can be shown equally well with a squeeze of the hand as with words. The bereaved sometimes takes advantage of this silence to unburden himself of the worries or fears that beset him or her.

Colin Murray Parkes

Fear of Being Misunderstood

Many dog owners clearly fear that their grief will not be taken seriously, afraid that society will find it unsuitable to mourn an animal, as opposed to a human being. And yet there are those who have been so distraught at the death of their pet that they have seriously considered suicide. But suicide is hardly something you talk about, especially if it were to be provoked by the death of an animal!

A deep emotional commitment to an animal is rather suspect and almost taboo in our culture. That is why many find it difficult to acknowledge such feelings. They are afraid that having a dog will be considered suspect, maybe a replacement for normal human contacts, even though a dog is usually only a complement in life — albeit a very important one.

If you really want to understand the grief of a dog owner, you therefore have to give up many preconceived notions regarding, for example, whom you are allowed to mourn and how. Those who themselves have lost a dog can fall back on their own experience. But even that may not be enough. What works for one may not work for everyone. It is therefore wise to be sparing with advice and instead listen and ask questions. Advice can also be proferred in the form of questions. A carefully phrased question is a way of showing confidence in the ability of the other to handle the situation and a way to activate his or her own resources.

Conversation

Here is an example of an imagined conversation. The background is this:

A woman, Anneli, called the medical emergency number in Gothenburg. She was worried about a headache — almost a migraine — that had been plaguing her day and night for almost a month. She had seen several doctors, but no one found anything wrong with her physically. Her headache kept increasing in strength and was often accompanied by nausea.

Anneli also mentioned that she had a very old and sick dog, and that she did not think it had much time left. This obviously added to her unhappiness. She asked if there was someone she might talk to about this. The nurse gave her my number.

Anneli: Hello. My name is Anneli. I got your number from the Medical Emergency. Did they tell you why I am calling?

Mickie: Hello. Yes, the nurse just called me. If I understood her correctly you are suffering from a terrible headache. And you evidently have dog who is not well.

Anneli: That's right. Do you have a few moments?

Mickie: Of course! I'll be happy to be of help. First I would like your phone number, though, so that I can call you back if we are cut off.

Anneli: I am very grateful that you want to listen to me. My number is . . .

Mickie: Tell me what happened, and what is worrying you.

Anneli: First of all, I have an excruciating headache. It started about a month ago. It got worse and worse, and today I can hardly stand up. Maybe it is because I have been crying so much today. My dog, Bliss, is old and sick and is getting worse and worse. Maybe the Emergency told you that?

Mickie: Yes, they did. What kind of dog is Bliss, and in what way is she sick?

Anneli: Bliss is a mutt, a bitch, twelve years old. She has age-related liver damage, and there is probably not be much that can be done about that. She is on a diet, but is just getting sicker and sicker. I have to walk her during the night and again early in the morning so that she can throw up.

Mickie: That doesn't sound good at all. When did she start throwing up?

Anneli: About two months ago. I got in touch with a vet who told me that she probably did not have long to go. It is terrible . . .

Mickie: Yes, it is always terrible to lose someone you love.

Anneli: Bliss means a lot to me, and I feel at loose ends. One moment she seems quite alert and then it feels impossible to say goodbye to her. The next moment she is so bad that I realize that something has to be done. And I'm so tired. I have a headache, I am dizzy and feel nauseated. I don't know how I am going to manage.

Mickie: What is it you don't know how you will manage?

Anneli: Having her put away. It feels terrible. And now when my head is hurting so much that I can hardly stand up, I can't even go to the vet with her.

Mickie: When did you say your headache started?

Anneli: About a month ago.

Mickie: And when did Bliss start to get sick?

Anneli: About two months ago. She has just got worse and worse the whole time.

Mickie: Do you think there might be a connection between your headaches and your anxiety and worrying about Bliss?

Anneli: I have asked myself the same thing. Could it be? I have heard that things like this might affect your sleep and your stomach. But can you get such an excruciating headache?

Mickie: I think it is quite possible that your headache is the result of everything you are going through right now. You are under a tremendous amount of stress and strain.

Anneli: Yes, it is hard. I hesitate between hope and despair the whole time. In a way, it would be a relief if that was what was causing my headache.

Mickie: They told me you have been to several doctors, but that no one could find anything wrong with you physically?

Anneli: Exactly. Next week I am going to yet another doctor for more tests. But I suspect that it might be tension and worry that are causing my headache and nausea.

Mickie: Probably. But it might be good to have it confirmed that it is nothing else. What are you going to do about Bliss?

Anneli: Bliss is still my greatest problem. My thoughts go round and round, but that may be part of it. She is on a diet, rice and fish and hamburger. I have friends whose dogs have the same kind of liver damage and they get only vegetarian food. Sometimes I wonder whether Bliss would improve if I gave her only vegetarian food. What do you think?

Mickie: It is hard for me to say. She might feel better, but the question is for how long? The answer obviously depends on how sick she is, among other things. Talk to your vet. He or she can probably give you an answer.

Anneli: Actually, there probably isn't much to be done, but you clutch at every little straw. I keep hoping . . . Bliss means so much to me . . . Have you ever been in a similar situation so you know what it feels like to lose a dog?

Mickie: Yes, I have. And it is as painful every single time.

Anneli: It is something you have to go through, as a dog owner, but you prefer not to think about it. Isn't it strange that you keep exposing yourself to hurts like these?

Mickie: Yes, it would seem so. But I guess that the dog adds so much to your life while it is alive that you are prepared to pay the price.

Anneli: We had many happy and close years together, Bliss and I. But now that the end is near, it is hard to admit it. I am still hoping for a miracle.

Mickie: It is understandable, and you should. And who can tell for sure, maybe there is more that can be done? Have you had her ever since she was a puppy?

Anneli: Yes, since she was six weeks. After that, it has almost always been just the two of us. Of course I have friends: I have many close friends, but there is something special about a dog. She is always around. It is so depressing to imagine life without her. It is not fair to have to decide whether she is to live or die. I feel like an executioner. To lead an innocent and trusting animal to death . . . She trusts me so much that she would follow me anywhere. How could I then decide to have her killed? It feels horrible and like an unforgivable betrayal of my best friend. Do you understand?

Mickie: Yes, I know exactly how you feel. You don't think it is up to you to decide over life or death?

Anneli: Exactly. And to make a decision like that in the case of Bliss, my best friend, is impossible.

Mickie: Try to look at it from another angle. Bliss is old and very sick. You who are closest to her is able to see to it that her suffering is not prolonged. In the case of human beings we cannot do that. All we can do is wait and try to ease their discomfort as much as possible. Although sometimes we wish that we could cut their suffering short. Thank God things are different with an incurable dog. We have the option of a dignified end, even if it is very hard. What you do, you don't do for your own sake, but for hers.

Anneli: Yes, it's true. I'll try to think that way. If I have the strength. If I am able to . . .

Mickie: I think it is important to level with yourself in a case like this and not blame yourself for what has to be done.

Anneli: It may also be true. It is not just the anxiety of having to decide about her life. I keep blaming myself for little things I have done to her. Sometimes I have been angry and impatient and stern. I keep thinking of a lot of things like that, and I am sorry and wish I hadn't done them. But it may be common to react like that, I don't know?

Mickie: Being overwhelmed by guilt is almost always part of grief. You blame yourself for a lot of little things that may assume enormous proportions later. But here too, you should be kinder to yourself and forgive yourself. Just think of how often you have been sweet and loving to Bliss, right?

Anneli: Yes, but I still don't think I'll ever forgive myself. I will have to learn to live with it.

Mickie: Yes, we'll have to learn.

Anneli: Another thing keeps bothering me a lot. Give me your advice? I don't know if I will be able to be there when Bliss is euthanized. If I cannot face it, my father will do it, he promised. Bliss likes him a lot and feels safe with him. But I don't know which is best.

Mickie: What do you feel like doing?

Anneli: I am afraid I can't take it. I may be so beside myself that Bliss may feel the same way, and I wouldn't want that under any circumstances.

Mickie: In that case, I think you had better not. Although I think you can master your feelings of anxiety in a situation like that much better than you think. All I can say is: do what you think best for both of you.

Anneli: Well, I'll see how I feel when the time comes. If I can't face it, my father will take care of it. You know, I actually feel a little better already. Just being able to talk about all the things that have been worrying me for so long. I already feel a bit calmer.

Mickie: I am happy I have been able to help you. Have you given some thought to what it will be like after Bliss? Do you have any plans?

Anneli: I don't think there will be any more dogs for me. It has been a never-ending thing of looking after the dog all these years. I live alone and work full time, and besides, I have irregular working hours. I have often thought it would be nice not to be so tied down, not to have to consider Bliss. Now that it is a fact, it just feels empty and lonely. I have actually been flirting with the idea of going somewhere for a couple of weeks, but I don't know when. It doesn't seem very tempting at the moment, but I realize at the same time that it would be a good thing to get away from home for a while.

Mickie: I can understand why you don't want to think about a trip just now. But as you say, it might be a good thing to get away from home and see something new. What you might do is to book your trip now but not leave until five or six weeks from now, or even later. If you book now, you are committed to a trip. Such a "commitment" may be precisely what is needed sometimes. You are not running away from reality. You have already confronted your grief. Coming back may be a painful reminder. But hopefully you will have gathered new strength by then.

Anneli: Actually it might not be a bad idea. I might do that. I have to tell you that I am really grateful to you for talking to me. Can I call you again if I need to?

Mickie: Of course. I'll be happy to hear from you.

Anneli: Thank you. It's good to know.

A week later I had a nice letter from Anneli telling me that she and Bliss had said goodbye.

Anneli Guided the Conversation

As you probably noticed, it was Anneli who guided the conversation and decided what she wanted to talk about. It is true that I led her thought to a future without Bliss. But not until Anneli seemed somewhat more composed.

The above is an example of an imaginary conversation. Naturally there are a number of variations. The main purpose is to point out and illustrate the discreet but nevertheless important role of the listener.

- Don't try to console. Words like "It could be worse" seem like a slap in the face under the circumstances. That is the last thing you want. Help children with their grief instead of trying to console them.

- Be close at hand. Show that you are available, that you are there, and that you sympathize. Have the courage to show your own grief and confusion.

- Listen actively. No advice — however well-meaning — will help. Listen, accept, confirm feelings. Share.

- Make physical contact. When you have nothing to say, holding someone's hand or hugging go a long way. Children who lack words can be held from behind so that their hands meet.

- Don't be afraid to cry. It is the body's way of expressing strong emotions. If you hold back, you also block feelings. Then they show up later, often several years later.

- Help find the words. Ask gently what happened, what they felt. One way of releasing grief is to put it in words. It is the useful first step in a grieving process.

- Don't run away. Make sure you stay. Leave your phone number to show that you are willing to continue your talk.

- Get back. Grief of this magnitude is not got rid of in one talk. Assume responsibility for finding out how things are. If you cannot see each other, write a brief note: "Thanks for the talk. I am thinking of you." It shows, in a concrete way, that your thoughts are there.

- When the bereaved tells you the same thing for the eleventh time, it is no help to hear you say: "You told me that before." Part of the grieving process consists of going over what has happened. When the process is completed these repetitions will cease.

- Be yourself. Don't try to be a psychologist or a priest or a teacher if you are not. We often hide behind our professional selves. The only things that counts here is compassion and caring.

Lennart Koskinen in *Expressen 1, Stockholm*. Advice after a tragic traffic accident with a high death toll.

Summary

- By being at hand, listening and showing respect and under-standing, we can contribute to making it easier for the bereaved.

- Offering condolences is not awkward or pushy. Avoiding the subject can be taken as a sign of lack of feeling or hardness.

- Calling, sending a card, flowers or a letter is always a thoughtful and kind gesture that warms the heart of those who mourn.

- It is more important than you think that friends and ac-quaintances openly show their sympathy to a pet owner who is mourning the death of his animal.

- Treat the privilege of sharing the grief of another with respect. Be careful about offering advice, especially cheer-ful and hearty statements.

Children's Grief

Lars was a shy and withdrawn nine-year old, a bit of a loner who found it very hard to establish contact with his contemporaries. His parents and teachers had long been discussing what they could do to help him "wake up" and become more active and involved in the world around him.

His mother, who probably was the one to suffer most from his loneliness and isolation, proposed one day that they get a dog. Her idea proved to even better than they expected. After the puppy's arrival, Lars started to change. His interest focused on nothing except the puppy and on caring for it. The more he learned about dogs, the more self-confident he became.

With great eagerness and interest, he began instructing his family in how to keep Adonis, as the dog was called, as happy and comfortable as possible. Before long, other children came to play with Lars and his dog. After only six months he was a perfectly normal child.

Time passed, and Adonis was two years old. And like many other dogs of that age he began to be somewhat difficult to handle. Everybody hoped that he would outgrow his problems. Instead the opposite happened, and finally the situation was completely out of hand.

I received a call from Lars' mother who asked me to help. My help was to consist of picking up Adonis right away, not to train him, but to take him to the vet to be euthanized!

Lars was not to be told. She thought it would be too hard on him. She and Lars would come to see me and leave the dog with me "for a vacation." She was hoping that Lars would take the loss less hard if he was told the truth later.

I am happy, both for the boy and for his parents, that this plan was never put into effect. A betrayal of that magnitude would probably have been very difficult to forget and forgive. Instead, we all got together and discussed the situation. Unfortunately, things were very bad. The problems had been allowed to become insurmountable.

After a number of attempts to train him, and after many discussions, the family decided on euthanasia. Lars participated in the decision, and nothing was decided behind his back. Naturally, he was next to inconsolable both before the act and for a long time afterwards. But at least he was given an honest chance to grieve — and he was not deceived! Lars lost his best friend, but not his confidence in his parents. They did not let him down, but allowed him to have his say. There was no escaping the pain, but his parents were there to share his grief.

Lars is fourteen now. And he still does not want another dog.

— When Adonis died, I didn't want another dog under any circumstances, he said, it would have been wrong. Now I am so busy that I don't have time for a dog, so it will have to wait. Although eventually I would like another dog — for Adonis was great . . .

A Lesson for Life

Losing a loved animal is an upsetting and traumatic experience, not only to us grown-ups, but even more so to children and young people. It is often their first confrontation with the transitory nature of life. Grief, the sense of loss and confusion provoke a multitude of important thoughts.

Young children often ask where the animal has gone, when it will be back, and why it is taking so long. The way those questions are answered may affect the way the child will be equipped to handle future crises and losses. If he is allowed to learn at an early stage that grief is something that must be accepted and discussed openly, the experience will become an important and valuable lesson for life.

Children's Reactions

The emotional pattern of a child losing someone close naturally resembles that of an adult in many ways. Certain reactions are more exaggerated in children, however, such as the fear of desertion, nightmares, sleeplessness, temper tantrums and difficulty with concentration.

Children also often experience pronounced feelings of guilt since, for obvious reasons, their ability to think rationally is not yet fully developed. Children sometimes express a desire to have the dog disappear or die. When then something happens, the death of the dog will be associated in their minds with this wish, and they may see the death of the dog as punishment for evil thoughts. Many also lack the ability to express their grief and fear in words.

If the parents have been less emotionally involved with the animal than the child, they may have a hard time realizing just how great

Children who are interested in caring for their animal and who enjoy its antics also become interested in what is happening around them. In order to provide better care for their animal, they are forced to become involved in their surroundings. Through mutual affection between children and animals, children become more reality-oriented and feel less cut off from their surroundings.

Ingemar Norling

the child's grief is. If they see the child bouncing back relatively quickly and seemingly without much difficulty, they are obviously happy and relieved. What they may not realize is that the child may be holding his grief back until the parents themselves say something. The child may be forced to carry and work on his grief alone and in silence.

We grown-ups often underestimate the importance of a dog to children. Consequently, we also have a hard time realizing the extent of the loss.

Children will look at their parents and draw their own conclusions from their behavior and reactions. The death of the dog will give rise to many questions in children, among them questions about his own death and how the parents would react to it. If the parents appear — in the eyes of the child — not to mourn a much loved animal, how would they then mourn the child if he were to die?

It may not be obvious to the child that they love him more than they loved the dog. The conclusion may be that they would not miss and mourn him any more than they did the dog. Children seldom express these thoughts and feelings openly, for one thing, because they are hard to put into words.

The actions and reactions of adults will teach children what norms prevail. They generalize what they learn, later applying it to other situations. To euthanize a dog — seemingly without too many qualms — just because it is regarded as "difficult" or "impossible," only to replace it with a new and "better" one, will teach children that it is morally right to get rid of difficult individuals and to replace them with others. Thoughts like these may lead to anxiety and insecurity in children. They have learned that difficult individuals have no worth, that they are unimportant.

Children and youngsters are often told by adults that they are impossible or difficult. Even if they do not conclude that the grown-ups intend to desert them, they experience, at close range, that a difficult individual is deserted and put to death.

Whenever a dog is euthanized for these reasons, it is of paramount importance that children be given as clear a picture of the situation as possible. If at all possible, they should be allowed to participate in discussions and decisions — always bearing in mind their age and level of development. Young children often find such discussions too complicated and inducing more anxiety than understanding and sense of security.

How to Ease the Pain of Children

The first question you ask yourself, as a parent, whenever a loved animal has died or has had to be put away, is how to break the news to the children. Most parents understandably think that children must be protected at all cost. Often this quite natural urge to spare them misses the mark, however, and the children are overprotected. They are deprived of the opportunity to prepare themselves and to handle their grief. At worst, you may risk an even more serious complication, namely that somewhat older children lose confidence in their parents because they feel lied to, betrayed and deceived.

It is always important to appeal to the children's reason and feelings. To tell a ten-year old, for example, that his dog has to be taken to the hospital for treatment and then have it euthanized unbeknownst to the child, is an obvious case of unforgivable betrayal from the child's point of view. He will obviously never be able to shrug off the fact that his parents had his best friend put to death.

Children are more capable of forming deep emotional bonds than we adults usually think. It is therefore dangerous to interpret silence as a sign that they have forgotten. They may very well be

Growing up with an animal who is well-adjusted and who is allowed to live according to its nature can be a rewarding experience to a child. An animal is part of life — moving, changeable, exciting as a playmate, maybe even a little dangerous.

An animal always adds an element of unpredictability to a home. . . . We are not able to sit down and make a plan for the little critters to follow — thank God . . .

Nor are we able to control how long our animal will be with us. One day we'll find Stina's rabbit stretched out stiffly on his side, his ears limp and his eyes glassy, flattened, a sorry sight to behold. What happened, was it frightened to death by a fox or a cat, did it catch a cold or did it eat something? Stina may never know the reason. But it is very important to allow her to work through her loss.

Stina arranged a real funeral. She put the rabbit in a shoe box, gently stroking its lifeless body, made a bed of tissue paper and put a lid on. On top of the lid she pasted a nice picture that she had made, carefully adding the birth and death dates of the rabbit. Then she went outside, accompanied by her solemn little brother to find a suitable place for the burial. Together they dug a deep hole and lowered the carton in it. Stina, her nose red, sang a little song, her little brother joining in occasionally. Then they shovelled the soil back, lovingly making a little round mound. They became quite excited at the thought of adding grass and flowers to the grave. This kept them busy all afternoon.

For the next few days, the family often talked about the rabbit, remembering how tiny and cute it was when they got it and all its antics throughout the years. At times they were overcome with grief, and Stina locked herself in her room, crying.

It would have been much harder for Stina had her mother tried to gloss over what happened to distract her thoughts and avoid talking about the rabbit. The death of a loved animal is a very real and important event in a child's life and should neither be overdramatized nor underestimated . . .

From the death of a pet many good things may come. If the family takes the event seriously, seeing to it that it worked it through thoroughly, it may serve to prepare the way for later and greater sorrows in children's lives.

From *Soft Animals* by Karin Neuschütz

harboring growing resentment towards their parents over their deceit.

We must allow children the opportunity to work on their grief in our company. By being open and honest, we are showing them that we trust them, that we respect their feelings and views and that they are worth listening and talking to — even about things that hurt and are hard. This attitude, when coming from their parents, will show children that they are respected and that they matter. It teaches them something very important, namely to trust others — not least their own parents.

Honesty and Understanding

Here are some suggestions as to what should and should not be done to make it easier for children to mourn:

- Answer children's questions honestly. Allow yourself time to explain things in terms that they will understand. Try to make children realize that, no matter how much we love someone and no matter what we do, there are situations in life that we are unable to control.

- Avoid explanations that may create increased anxiety and worry, for example: "The dog is sleeping." This can give rise to mounting fear of falling asleep, since it may mean that you will die.

- "The dog didn't like it here so it left us." This may give rise to severe feelings of guilt and regrets.

- "The dog was sick and died." An expression such as this may result in an exaggerated fear of illness. If you explain that the dog died from a disease, you have to add that the animal was extremely sick. Otherwise children may think that the slightest sickness may result in death.

- "The dog was so sick that the veterinarian had to put it to death." This statement, without further explanation, can only be interpreted in a negative way.

- Tell children that grief is unfortunately not rare, something that everyone will experience when they lose someone they love. This assurance will offer a certain comfort when children are confronted with their own painful thoughts and feelings.

- Allow children to show and act out their feelings openly, no matter how irrational. Children should be encouraged to vent their worries, their disappointments and their despair and not learn to suppress and bury such emotions.

- Don't inhibit their feelings and expressions of grief by saying "big boys and girls don't cry" or "it was only a dog, we can easily get another."

- Make it easier for children to grieve by helping them handle their grief. You may ask questions, look at pictures of the dog or talk about the past. You can also encourage them to draw pictures, write poems or an essay about their pet and about how it feels to lose a friend.

- Ask the children whether they have any special wishes regarding the funeral or some other form of farewell ceremony. If at all possible, try to fulfill their wishes. The funeral or other farewell ceremony is an important aspect of the grieving process to many children — and adults.

- Tell their teacher about their loss — this for several reasons. By telling the teacher about important events outside school you afford him or her the opportunity to be more observant, tactful or tolerant towards the children. Without this piece of information, it is easy to misinterpret possible lack of concentration, bad mood or other reactions. If the teacher possesses this information, he or she will be able to alert the parents to any reaction that they may otherwise not be aware of. An understanding teacher may use the tragic event to conduct a classroom discussion on what it is like to lose someone you love. Such lessons can be extremely valuable to the students. Children may be made to realize that grief is something that hits everybody.

- Never put pressure on children by starting to talk about replacing the dog with another. It is usually wise to wait a while. Most children are not at all ready to find a quick replacement for their dog.

- Be aware of your own feelings and reactions to the death of the dog. Even if you yourself do not happen to be particularly affected, you should try to put yourself in the children's place which may be quite different from your own. If you honestly mourn the dog, do not be afraid to show it.

- Allow yourself time to listen to the children. Show them that you understand and that you care.

Our first task as parents or as a friend wanting to help children in their grief is to reassure them that their reactions are completely normal. Then encourage their questions, accept the expression of their sorrow, provide honest answers and explanations and, last but not least, let your own behavior provide a positive example for your children to follow.

By acting in this way we are helping our children through a difficult period in life at the same time as we are teaching them something important. You will provide the foundation for handling and countering future disappointments, crises and grief in the best possible way.

Summary

- Children and young people are extremely observant when it comes to attitudes and reactions of grown-ups. From this they learn which norms apply in life.

- It is important not to be overprotective. Let children share — in a way suited to their age — in the difficulties and sorrows that are unavoidable in life.

- Children have an excellent memory. They are capable of stronger emotional attachments than we give them credit for.

- Children's questions should always be answered frankly and openly in words they understand.

- For the sake of the children's grieving process and their continued development it is important that they be encouraged to show their feelings openly.

- Having someone who listens, comforts and cares is obviously every bit as important to children and young people as it is to us adults.

Grief and Loss from Other Causes

Yvonne referred to herself and her dog Lollo as the fixtures of Canine Consultants, since they had participated in practically every activity we offered. They had taken every class and mastered every single skill.

To us, Yvonne was a wonderful representative of the Perfect Dog Owner. It was not so much her immense expertise as her loving relationship to her dog that aroused our admiration, however.

— When I got Lollo, I had no idea how time-consuming it is to have a dog, said Yvonne. But the time I devote to making sure that Lollo is well and happy also makes me happy with life in general.

Dogs and humans are two different species. Lollo had her playmates and Yvonne wanted hers. She met a man and they got married. They formed a family which eventually grew to include yet another member, a little baby. Yvonne now divided her affection between her husband, child and dog. With time, the family also came to include a business venture of their own.

That was when we noticed that Yvonne was worn out. She still kept up her training sessions with Lollo, but no longer with the same degree of enthusiasm. She was exhausted. We realized that she had to do something about this, and knew that it would not be easy. The problem was more than simply cutting down on the time devoted to Lollo.

Finally, after long deliberations and many qualms, she decided that Lollo needed a new home.

A number of different problems presented themselves. Who could be counted on to provide the same quality life for Lollo that she had become accustomed to with Yvonne?

Yvonne constantly had a bad conscience and felt over extended. The whole idea behind a new home for Lollo was that she no longer would be neglected.

Now the hunt started for a new home for Lollo. Meanwhile, Yvonne was beset upon by friends and relatives.

— You should have Lollo put away instead, they said. You will never be sure how she is. It would be better for her to be put to sleep for good.

This was no solution to Yvonne, however. Lollo was still a young dog, strong and hopefully still had many years ahead of her.

We looked high and low for a new home for Lollo, at our wit's end. Where could we find a home equal to Yvonne's demands?

Then one day we found a family with two teenagers who wanted to care for Lollo. To our delight, Yvonne and the new family took an instant liking to each other, as did Lollo and the family. Yvonne visited the new home. She made sure that she would be allowed to see Lollo from time to time in the future. When it was time to say goodbye, the family came to pick up Lollo whom they knew quite well by now. Lollo went with them willingly and happily. With a heavy heart, Yvonne sadly watched Lollo disappear. Life would not be the same without Lollo, that she knew.

A month later Yvonne and Lollo met in the home of the new family. Yvonne had waited a month to give Lollo time to adjust. After the visit she called us and told us enthusiastically about her pleasure at seeing Lollo again.

— She is well, you can tell, she said. We took a long walk, and it was great. It felt the same as always. When I had to give her back I naturally had a lump in my throat. But when I watched her climb up in the sofa, putting her head on her new mistress' lap I knew I had done the right thing. She is fine. They love her, and she seems to be more harmonious than with me towards the end. But it still hurts to see her seeking somebody else's company. I know I am being very selfish. Lollo is happy and that's what counts. When I came home I felt a little better, even though I miss her terribly. For the first time in a whole month I felt almost happy.

We did not hear from Yvonne for a while. We ignored our misgivings, telling ourselves that she was probably very busy, and that actually, she no longer had a reason to get in touch. Nevertheless, it did feel a bit empty.

Then one day, about two months later, an extremely upset and almost desperate Yvonne came rushing to our office.

— I can't stand it any longer, she sobbed. Then her voice faltered.

When she had recovered a little, she said:

— In the beginning, when we discussed the idea of a new home, I told you about the reactions of my family. Everybody told me to have Lollo euthanized. They said that I would never be able to be sure how she was getting along in another house. I didn't listen then, but now things are getting worse. I feel completely worthless. I haven't even had the strength to visit Lollo. Every time I mention her — and I do quite often — everyone tells me that I did the wrong thing. Before long I won't know what is right and what is wrong. Everytime I miss her they say: You have yourself to blame! It is as if I am not allowed to miss her if she is still alive, only if she is dead!

We talked about her guilt feelings for a long time, and about the grief she still experienced. She blamed herself for being insufficient, and she was beside herself for having felt obliged to opt for separation. Her guilt and anxiety were constantly fuelled by uncaring and judgmental people around her.

Eventually Yvonne's feelings of guilt and aggression subsided. But the past few years would have been so much easier had she had a more understanding and supportive husband. Today, she remains convinced that she did the right thing, in spite of everything.

— Lollo is alive and well off, she says. And that is the only thing that matters, after all.

Having to give up a still living dog as Yvonne did, may be every bit as painful as losing it through death. Regardless of the reasons, all separation evokes strong feelings of desertion, emptiness, guilt and aggression. In this situation, the mourner is always dependent on a caring and understanding environment.

Voluntary Separation

It may be misleading to use the word "voluntary" here, since it implies that you give up your dog willingly. Actually, it is more that you find yourself in a situation where you are forced to give up the dog. It is voluntary only in the sense that alternatives exist, and that you have some degree of say-so about the separation.

Having to give up your dog while it is still alive, no matter how justified it may be, induces strong feelings of guilt — not only towards the dog but towards the surroundings.

Having to choose between keeping your dog and something else may lead to feelings of anger and disappointment at being forced to make such a choice. It may also entail self-reproach at having chosen to give up your pet.

There are romantic stories about the affection of dogs and their sadness at losing their owners. There are tales about dogs who cover enormous distances in order to find their former owner, and about dogs who have lain down to die on the grave of their owner. There are stories about dogs who refuse to eat or grieve to death . . .

There is no doubt that dogs have a great ability to show their owners great affection. Interpreting such fondness as deep-seated affection of a "human" kind, is obviously flattering to the object of this "love." But it can also lead to the mistaken idea that the dog will mourn us the same way as we humans may mourn at a separation. The dog is by nature a herd animal. This means, among other things, that it is easier to form attachments to several individuals than to one at any given time. Furthermore, the dog is better able to adjust to new situations than we imagine.

A dog who has a new owner adjusts readily, transferring its affection to the new care-giver as long as he or she fulfills its needs. It does not miss its old owner in the human way that we think — or like to imagine.

A dog does not forget its old owner, however. If they meet again, it shows its joy at seeing a well-known person. But unlike a human being, a dog has the enviable ability to live entirely in the here and now. It lacks the ability to torment itself by mourning and grieving the way we do.

It is the human who suffers when a new home has to be found for a dog. It is the owner who keeps wondering, pining and worrying. The dog will be happy and will adjust quite easily provided it has found a good home. Considerate people therefore prefer a new home to having the dog euthanized.

If you make this choice, it is most important that you weigh your motives and considerations carefully until you are completely convinced that you have made the best possible decision for the dog, for yourself and for your family.

A New Home

Unfortunately, many remain unconvinced that their dog will be able to adjust to a new home — so they have it put away.

They argue that being dead is better for the dog than being cared for by somebody else. For some reason, every pet owner considers himself or herself most capable and competent to care for his or her pet.

They worry about whether the new family or new care-giver

will really love the dog as much as they did. Will the dog receive the same consideration and attention? Will it still be allowed to get up in bed? Will the new family continue to give it the loving pats that it has grown accustomed to? Will it get its nightly snacks and its walks?

In your anxiety, it is easy to overlook that there are others who might give the dog as good a — possibly even better — home as you yourself had to offer.

Suggestions and Helpful Hints

Here are some helpful hints on how to find a good home for the dog if necessary:

- First ask around among family and friends who know your dog to see whether someone would be willing to take it. It would obviously be nice if you were allowed to see the dog from time to time in the future. It won't hurt the dog. If the dog already knows his new care-giver, so much the better for both.

- Mention to your veterinarian that you are looking for a new home for your dog. Vets often come into contact with people who want a grown dog, for various reasons. Your chances of finding the right person that way are very good.

- Get in touch with an organization, club or person devoted to finding new homes for pets. Reserve the right to inspect the new home and visit the dog after some time has passed.

- Many have found a good home for their dog through an ad.

- If you are considering handing your dog over to someone you don't know, first pay a visit to his home and make sure you will be allowed to visit the dog in the future. Draw up a written agreement safeguarding this right. Observe the behavior of the other family members towards the dog, as well as their attitudes towards animals in general. If you have the slightest doubt about the suitability of the family, you should not turn over your dog. Instead, try again. A new placement should feel right and be based on mutual trust.

- If you are pressed for time and have to find a new home for your dog within a certain period of time, don't wait until the last minute. Remember that it might be difficult to find a suitable person who is prepared to open his home to a grown animal.

Involuntary Separation

There are situations and circumstances beyond the control of even the most responsible dog owner, such as the dog escaping, never to reappear, while your back is turned.

This not only gives rise to unhappiness about the loss, but also to a multitude of questions about what might have happened. Was it stolen, or did it leave on its own?

What is not known sets the imagination in motion, so you usually assume the very worst. You imagine your dog, homeless, hungry or possibly hurt or killed in an accident. The idea that it may be safe and well cared for seems out of the question.

Guilt, Aggressiveness and Search

Whenever a dog disappears mysteriously and inexplicably, we naturally respond with both anger and feelings of guilt. And of course we try to find the dog.

Long after giving up all hope of ever finding the dog we may imagine that we glimpse it somewhere.

If the dog was stolen, it is natural that we feel very bitter and angry that someone might be so cruel and purposely cause another human being such pain. You are extremely angry — and your anger is justified — but there is no one to vent it on. Therefore it is often directed at yourself. "I should not have let the dog out of my sight for a moment. I should have guarded against the possibility of someone stealing it. I should have thought."

This kind of self-reproach can haunt you for years to come.

> Guilt is nothing more than worries about the past — it is being paralyzed now about something that happened in the past. The degree of action paralysis may range from simple upset to serious depression.
>
> Guilt feelings are unhealthy, because you expend your present energy ineffectively by feeling hurt, upset or depressed about something that is past history. It is both senseless and unhealthy.
>
> Wayne W. Dyer

Anger makes your grief worse, and it may sometimes be more intense than that caused by any other kind of loss.

It is important, as always when you blame yourself for something, that you look at what actually happened and try to understand it.

Are your guilt feelings justified?

If they are, you have to try to accept your guilt and then forgive yourself.

All grief includes an element of search. Even though you may be well aware that the one you grieve is dead, you still continue your search more or less subconsciously.

If your dog has disappeared, you naturally search for it. This search is rational and justified. For if you don't search for it actively, our chances of ever seeing the dog again are very slight.

The hardest thing is probably to know when to stop searching and accept that the dog is gone. But this is precisely what you have to do after a while, or you risk delaying and aggravating your grieving process. You will be caught in a painful pattern of "eternal search."

What Can Be Done

If your dog disappears you must act immediately. The longer you wait the less chance of ever finding it. Here are some things you can do:

- Get in touch with the police and all animal shelters, veterinary clinics and animal hospitals in the area where you live. If someone claims to have your dog and is able to describe it, go there immediately. If it turns out not to be your dog, you must continue your search. Go back to the animal shelters every other day if you can. Also, put up notices everywhere.

- Since most lost dogs are found close to where they disappeared, concentrate your search to that area. Talk to guards, store owners and others who live or work in the area.

- Go from door to door in the area where you think your dog disappeared. Give out your telephone number. Ask people to call you if they think they have found your dog or have some information. Don't forget to mention a reward. It makes people interested in participating actively.

- Post a reward. The offer of a reasonable amount may be the decisive factor in persuading someone to return your dog.

- Make a poster, large enough to be seen but not so large that it will be difficult to place. The notice should mention color, breed, sex and any special identifying marks, as well as the time and place where the dog disappeared and your telephone number. If the dog is on medication, please list the kind of medication, the dose and what symptoms may arise in the absence of medication. Have a suitable number of posters made. Ask friends and acquaintances to help post the notices where lots of people pass by, e g stores, bus stops, telephone booths, post offices, banks, veterinary clinics, etc.

- Put an ad in the dailies. The ad may contain the same information as the poster. Also read the "Found" ads.

- Make sure you can be reached by phone or ask somebody else to watch your phone. If someone calls and claims to have seen your dog, first ask for his name and address and then for other information. Have him describe the dog. Otherwise you may ask leading questions and thus get the answers you want, although they may be false.

Arrange to meet the person at his or her place. If you are at all suspicious, arrange to meet in a neutral and public place. It may be wise to take a friend along.

• Don't forget to remove the posters once your dog has been found!

Summary

• Being separated from a still living dog may be every bit as painful as losing it through death.

• Finding a new home — as an alternative to euthanasia — is usually the best solution — for all parties concerned.

• When placing the dog in a new home, it is not the dog that is subject to longing, pining and grieving. Animals have the blessed capacity to live in the here and now.

• When an animal disappears mysteriously and inexplicably, it always gives rise to strong feelings of guilt, bitterness and anger.

• The hardest thing about losing a close friend — no matter how — is accepting what has happened. This may be harder and take longer if the animal has disappeared without explanation.

Welcoming a New Dog

Börje retired two years ago and has now been able to devote much of his time to his dog. Actually, he and his wife shared Emma, as the dog was called, but since Börje loved to take long walks it was his task to walk Emma.

Emma was old and frail, and finally Börje had to say goodbye to his old friend. His home, which he shared with his wife Margit, grew quiet.

The master — no longer anybody's master — tried to keep up his long walks anyway, but they were neither as much fun nor as long as when he had been accompanied by Emma. After a while he gave them up, and mostly stayed at home. Margit, who also missed Emma, but who seemed to have weathered the loss better, got more and more worried about his "couch potato" life, as she called it. She shared her concern with her two grown sons.

Börje and Margit had actually not wanted another dog. While Emma was still alive, they had talked about how much fun it would be to do some traveling before they were too old. But their sons were convinced that a new dog was the answer.

Three months after Emma's death Pelle, the new puppy, arrived on the scene — to Börje's considerable surprise and annoyance. There was no doubt that it was a surprise. Börje, who was frank and open, did not mince his words. He was furious. Without even glancing at the puppy, he rushed to the front door, grabbed his coat, hurled some well chosen words in Margit's direction before slamming the door behind him.

Two hours later he was back and, without saying a word, he sat down, staring at the poor, uncomprehending puppy. Then he fixed Margit with his eyes as if she had committed an unpardonable sin.

— What do you mean by this? he said.

— I really wanted another dog, she lied, hoping that he would calm down.

And he did — eventually. With great hesitation on his part and after many discussions, they finally decided to let the puppy stay.

By the time the pup was six months old it had become a terrible nuisance. That was when I met the family for the first time and heard the story of what had happened.

Instead of training Pelle, we talked. It took several sessions before Börje and Margit had sorted out how they really felt. Neither of them actually wanted a dog. Margit admitted to Börje that she had agreed to their sons' suggestions out of concern for him.

Now they had a dog that nobody wanted, and whom they could not really take to. They both agreed that Pelle was a nice little guy — although obviously not the same as Emma! They kept him only because they did not know what to do with him.

— We cannot have the poor thing put to death. It is not his fault, but nor do we seem to learn to love him, Börje said.

It was a difficult situation, not least for Pelle who, sensitive like all dogs, was negatively affected by the whole thing. He became restless, anxious and disobedient. Margit and Börje wrestled with feelings of responsibility and guilt, made worse by reluctance and indecision. They felt sorry for Pelle, but their hearts still belonged to Emma.

We talked about finding a new home, and Margit thought it might be a good solution. Börje hesitated and finally suggested:

— Let's keep Pelle a little while longer. We'll do our best and try to learn to like him. Maybe it will be easier once we realize how important our love is to him. For it is not Pelle's fault that it is this way. If we really try, but still don't make it, we'll find a new home for him. At that point we will at least know that we tried!

Börje registered Pelle in a training class for puppies. Not just for Pelle's sake, but also because they wanted to be with other dog owners.

— Maybe we'll feel like real dog owners again, Börje said.

Little by little Margit and Börje grew fond of their dog. Six months later there was no talk of finding a new home for him.

— Imagine, Margit said on one occasion, it took us a full year to learn to accept him and like him. A whole year! And he who is so wonderful! We must have been blind!

It takes time, as in the case of Margit and Börje, to sort out your feelings, to work through your grief, to prepare for the eventuality of another dog, and to decide if and when you are ready to welcome a new animal. The most important thing to consider is whether you are emotionally ready to involve yourself with a new individual.

Even if the thought of another dog presents itself right away, it may still be wise to wait a while and consider a number of other factors — ranging from your feelings for the dog you lost, to the pros and cons of another one.

Confusion and Indecision

The stronger your ties to the dead dog, the harder it may be to replace it with another. You may notice that you cannot help make comparisons between the two — and that the new dog naturally will come out the loser. Maybe you worry about not being able to become emotionally involved with the new dog the way you should.

This fear is often justified, since the dead dog is still very much alive in your mind. If you ignore these misgivings and decide on a new dog anyway, you may find yourself facing some problems. On the one hand, you are unable to muster up any fondness for the newcomer. On the other, you blame yourself for being both cold and unfair, because you are not able to engage yourself as deeply as you should. In this case, the best solution is often to find another home for the new dog.

Many are unfortunately not aware of how hard it usually is to transfer your affection to a new dog. You mostly think of how much fun it will be to have a dog in the house.

What you actually want is to continue to have a dog — the old dog. You are still not ready to get involved with a new one.

You are neither over your grief nor have you accepted your loss or sorted out what you really want.

The story below is an example of what might happen if you get a new dog without sufficient thought to the consequences.

Cita and her Mistress

A woman came to see me about her "terribly fearful and difficult" German shepherd bitch. She was afraid that the dog might become aggressive with time, since it had these tendencies at the tender age of six months.

Cita, as the dog was called, turned out to be a little bundle of energy, with sparkling eyes, always on the lookout for new adventures. If what her mistress had in mind was a companion to share her quiet evenings at home she may have been on the lively side, but Cita was, after all, still a pup.

Cita had absolutely no fear of humans. If she had to choose between coming to see you or continuing what she was doing at the moment, she did not hesitate for a moment when offered some goodies and sweet talk. "Bribes" her mistress contemptuously called them.

Obedience was not her strong side, but she was, after all, still a puppy — and not an especially well brought up one at that. Whenever her mistress called: "Come here" she took off — in the opposite direction.

When the leash was brought out, and it was time for a walk, the same pattern of behavior was always repeated. Cita ran straight towards her mistress at full speed, and then veered to the right or to the left right in front of her. The chase was on. The playful Cita was chased round and round by her far from happy mistress.

When Cita was scolded, she always behaved in a special way. She bounced up and down, ran the whole length of the leash, throwing herself sideways, this way and that. She seemed intent on trying to assuage her mistress and make her change her mind.

When she finally grew tired of fun and games, she tried to climb up in somebody's lap, with all the persistence of an affectionate dog — however, usually not in that of her mistress.

This was Cita: affectionate, playful, unafraid and showing absolutely no signs of aggressiveness towards anything or anyone.

In other words, a completely ordinary charming puppy, full of happy mischief. Why then did her mistress find fault with her?

When you watched Cita and her mistress together, it was obvious that Cita's disobedience and liveliness were more pronounced in the company of her mistress than in the company of others. There was also a touch of restlessness to her playfulness. When she tried to establish contact with her mistress through her various antics and games, there was an element of anxiety and hesitation in her behavior. It was if she did not quite know how to behave.

If Cita wanted pats and hugs, she did not first go to her mistress but to somebody else in the vicinity.

Since Cita's behavior around other people was almost exemplary, it seemed natural to look for the roots of her behavior in her relationship to her mistress. The most noteworthy thing was the total absence of pats and praise from her mistress. After several visits, she had not once shown Cita any form of approval or kindness. "Fie!" and "No!" and a jerk at the leash was the usual reaction. Whenever someone said something nice about Cita, her mistress seemed almost put out or annoyed.

This made me wonder. Why did this woman seek my help with a puppy that she actually did not care for at all? And why did she become annoyed at the slightest sign of progress in Cita or if anyone had a good word for Cita? Why was she so reluctant to try any of the methods I suggested? The questions kept piling up.

Finally I had to take the bull by his horns and ask her why she was so cold-hearted and rejecting. Her immediate reaction was to deny that this was the case. Then she started to tell me about her old dog.

Vanja had been obedient and nice, beautiful and calm, in other words the exact opposite of Cita who was always clamoring for her attention. Vanja had been her faithful companion for twelve years, completely attuned to her habits and her moods. They had been a tightly knit couple — in fact, there had probably never been a dog with as well-developed a personality, so quiet, so harmonious, so obedient, so, well, close to perfect. When Vanja died, her life became so empty and so depressing that she acquired Cita already after a week to "take Vanja's place."

Comparing a puppy to a twelve-year old well-known, much loved dog will obviously never work in the puppy's favor. In her blind desire for company, the woman had chosen to ignore this obvious fact. There was no room in her heart for Cita, as long as she was engaged in mourning Vanja.

Since it was clear that she was not ready to change her attitude towards Cita, I suggested finding a new home for her as a last resort. For I was completely convinced that, given the right care, Cita would grow up to become a harmonious and well-adjusted dog. I emphasized that a new home would give her mistress the satisfaction of knowing that Cita would have a chance of a rich and meaningful life. And she would not have to blame herself or feel that she had somehow failed.

But she would not be persuaded. There was no way of knowing what Cita's new home would be like, but she promised to think the matter over. Four days later Cita was put to death — for being mentally deficient.

Many of us were saddened by Cita's fate. She paid a high price for the insensitivity and pigheadedness of her mistress.

New Dog or Not

There is every reason to consider the individual circumstances, both for your own sake and for those of the dog.

It could be that the children were the ones who originally wanted a dog. After they grew up and moved away from home there may no longer be the same motivation to care for another dog. Maybe your working conditions have changed, so that you no longer have time or space to get as involved as you did with the old dog. Maybe interests or the family situation have changed, so that another dog might actually be more of a nuisance than a source of joy.

It is also of utmost importance that you sort out your feelings towards the old dog. Are these still so strong and your grief so alive that they would come between you and the new animal?

It is quite common that people are burdened by guilt feelings towards the deceased pet. Acquiring another dog feels like an act of betrayal. These guilt feelings may act as an invisible barrier, preventing you from welcoming the new animal wholeheartedly.

To many, the loss of a beloved dog is so traumatic and represents such a shock to the system that they do not dare commit themselves to a new one. In that case, you should hold off for the time being. It goes without saying that it is not possible to have an animal that you want to enjoy, at the same time as you, more or less subconsciously, keep it at arm's length emotionally.

Since the whole idea of owning an animal is to develop a relationship which will last for many years and which will be mutually rewarding, there is every reason to consider whether you are truly ready. Here are some questions that may help you to face this important decision:

- Are you so far along in your grief work that you are ready to enter a new relationship without reservation? Would it feel as an act of betrayal to your old dog if you replaced it with another?

- Are you able to treat your new dog as a completely separate, unique individual, and not make comparisons and look for similarities with the old one?

- Is your need for a dog as strong today as it was when you acquired the old one? Or are you contemplating getting another dog mainly out of habit?

- Do you have the same amount of time and interest to devote to the new dog as you had when you acquired your old one?

- Are you prepared to commit yourself to the time and amount of care that the dog will require, or would you prefer to remain free and not tied down for a while?

- Are you primarily looking for something else to occupy your thoughts instead of devoting all your time to grieving the dog you lost?

- Would life without a dog become too empty and meaningless? Is it important to your quality of life that you have a dog?

Talk the matter over with others, naturally first and foremost with your family. If children are affected by your decision, it is obviously important that they be heard. If opinions are divided within the family, you may have every family member write down his or her opinion of the advantages and disadvantages of a dog. Once their thoughts are down on paper, it is easier to discuss them and look at the problem more objectively.

If you have no family to consult, close friends may be helpful.

It is very easy, as a parent, to get a new dog out of the best intentions, without first consulting the child. Even though your intention may be the very best and strictly based on your desire to ease the child's grief, things may nevertheless turn out the wrong way.

Older children may refuse to acknowledge the dog. To them it may feel like betraying the old dog. They need plenty of time to complete their grieving process and to start preparing for owning a new dog. Although they may be looking forward to owning another dog eventually, you may do well to wait until they bring the matter up themselves.

Young children often react to the death by wanting another dog right away. They obviously need consoling. Their first wish may therefore be for a new "animal to cuddle." As a parent you have an important mission as comforter. For it is comforting that the child needs — not necessarily another dog right away.

If the dead dog is replaced by a new one too soon, the child's grief work will be interrupted. Trying to handle grief is an important lesson for life. If the child gets the idea that a loved one may be replaced right away, he will get the wrong notion concerning what emotional commitment is. As an adult, he will handle grief and separation the way he learned as a child. If he was taught that someone close may easily be replaced by another, he will be in for needless difficulties and disappointments later in life.

Of course there are situations where waiting makes no sense. It may neither be advisable nor possible to wait in the case of a

person living alone and who may be completely dependent on a dog to give life meaning, or in the case of someone who depends on his or her dog for practical assistance.

Trying to Bridge Sorrow

Many watch the aging process in their dog with anxiety and start to think of a replacement while the old dog is still alive.

They think that having a young dog around will ease the pain when the old one dies — which is far from certain. Your grief may be every bit as intense no matter how many animals you have. Naturally, it is affected by the intensity of the attachment to the old dog: if it was very strong, your grief and sense of loss will also be deep. In this case, a new dog will neither be able to replace the old one or lighten your sorrow and loneliness.

Sometimes there are problems when a new dog arrives on the scene, and sometimes there are no complications whatsoever.

In the first case, the established dog accepts the newcomer who, in his turn, quickly adjusts to the new circumstances. But if things don't work out, a troublesome competition can develop between the two dogs, with the old and established dog constantly asserting his dominance and guarding his territory. The newcomer is forced to fight for his place and position.

The old dog, in its turn, may find it stressful and threatening to have a newcomer competing for its favorite chair and attention time. Is this fair either to the old dog or to the newcomer or to yourself?

Advice and Guidelines

Here are some ideas and some advice to facilitate the introduction of a new dog into your home:

- Do not view getting a new dog as an act of betrayal towards your old dog. On the contrary, it shows that the earlier relationship was so rewarding that you are willing to try it again.

- The newcomer is a stranger. Don't expect the new dog to adjust to strange and alien surroundings right away.

- Allow yourself and your family plenty of time to adjust to the newcomer. See to it that you are allowed to get to know the new dog and its unique personality in peace and quiet.

- Do not expect the new dog to behave exactly as the old one. Try another breed, and avoid giving the dog the same name as its predecessor.

- Discover the new dog's unique personality. Register differences rather than similarities with the old one.

- Allow yourself to remember, miss and grieve the dead dog. This is especially important if the new dog arrived in your home shortly after the death of the other. Do not try to escape your feelings, and above all, do not feel guilty about them — it may prolong the grieving process.

- If, in spite of all your efforts, you should discover that the new dog does not work out, try to find a new home for it. Don't regard it as a failure, but be thankful that you were able to acknowledge that the relationship was untenable. Things may change, and you may be ready to try again with another dog.

Summary

- It is important to have most of your grief behind you before getting another dog. Otherwise the new dog may have to live in the shadow of a memory with which it will never be able to compete successfully.

- If you are the least bit hesitant about getting a new dog, you should take it as a warning sign that you are not yet ready for it.

- A new dog can neither replace the old dog nor absorb your thoughts to such a degree that you forget your grief and loss.

- There are times when getting a new dog right away is the only thing to do.

- Successful new dog ownership is not just a matter of filling a void. Above all, it requires that you are prepared and willing to commit all your love and affection to the new relationship.

Epilogue

We have all asked questions about the meaning of life: Who am I? Where do I come from? Where am I going? Why am I here, and what is death? Is there an existence beyond the body? Will I keep returning in new guises to learn new lessons? Will we meet again?

For some, the answers are given, while most of us keep asking, questioning, doubting and seeking.

When our lives flow calmly and smoothly without being jolted by dramatic events, we fill our days with work and our leisure time with pleasure and pastimes of all kinds. These eternal questions do not seem very important then.

But when we find ourselves in the midst of a serious crisis in life, for instance when someone we love deeply and dearly dies, the questions immediately return with renewed insistence and intensity, demanding an answer.

A dog owner is no exception. Who was it actually that died?, he may ask. Was it my dog — or just his body? Does a dog have a soul, like we humans do, or. . . ?

In the course of grief or any other major crisis, our senses temporarily play tricks on us. People and things appear strangely dreamlike and hazy — not quite real. In moments like these we are at our most receptive to inner turmoil.

Grief opens our innermost senses. Grief makes us reach out towards an inner reality in order to arrive at answers to these mysteries. Both our inner resources and obvious truths which we otherwise never come close to, may be released in the darkness of grief.

Let us take advantage, with humility, of these exalted moments of insight and truth.

Your joy is your grief unmasked.

The same source, whence your laughter bubbles, has often been filled with tears.

How might it be otherwise?

The more you are made hollow by grief, the more joy you are able to contain.

Is not the cup which holds your wine the very cup which was fired in the potter's kiln?

Is not the lute that sooths your spirit the same piece of wood that was hollowed out with knives?

When you are happy, look deeply into your hearts and you will find that only that which has brought you grief now brings you joy.

When you are sad, look again into your heart and you will see that you are actually weeping over that which once brought you joy.

Some of you will say: "Joy is greater than grief," and others will say "No, grief is greater."

But I say to you that they are inseparable.

They come together, and when one of them dines alone with you, the other is sleeping in your bed.

In truth, you are like a pair of scales balanced between your grief and your joy. You are still and in balance only when the scales are empty. When the Treasurer lifts you up in order to weigh his gold or his silver, then your joy or your grief must either rise or fall.

Kahil Gibran

Guide to Further Study
By Nina Roegner

Mickie Gustafson wrote *Just a Dog* primarily as a guide for those who face the grieving process that follows the loss of a pet or for those who already find themselves in the midst of this process. She is also addressing herself to the family and friends of the bereaved as well as the veterinary staff and others concerned.

This subject has a bearing on all pet owners sooner or later. Her book is therefore useful as a point of departure and source of inspiration for further exploration. By addressing these difficult issues ahead of time, the animal owner is not left unprepared for when grief strikes.

The author stresses the vital importance of the immediate surroundings. It is to be hoped that this book will inspire family, friends, veterinary personnel and others concerned to acquaint themselves with the course of the grieving process. In this way, those close to the bereaved may actively and lovingly contribute to turning grief work into an enriching and rewarding process instead of, as is unfortunately often the case, one which gives rise to bitter memories.

In some cases, professional help is needed to help the bereaved through his or her grief. This book may be helpful in deciding if and when the intervention of a psychologist, minister etc. might be called for.

Multi-function Role

The study guide is primarily designed for study circles or group discussions, but can obviously be used for self-directed study. Group activity is designed to provide:

- Greater insight into the grieving process which all pet owners must undergo at some point,

- Awareness of the possibilities for personal development which may result from well managed grief work,

- Frequent opportunities to discuss the situation from the point of view both of the animal and the bereaved, and to explore the attitudes and actions of the surroundings.

Every study group will work according to its own needs and conditions. The purpose of the study guide is to serve as a resource for ideas, hints and suggestions on how to proceed. The study guide must never be allowed to determine the course of the discussion.

The participants must contribute their own experiences and views. Below are 63 suggested topics for group discussion.

How to Conduct a Study Group

The leader should be capable of guiding the discussion, delegating tasks and convening the group.

After preparing for the task, anybody may serve as leader for the group. The leader must scrutinize carefully any literature selected, as well as the study guide and any other material deemed appropriate to the group's activities.

Course Literature

The basic material consists of *Losing Your Dog* which must be made available to all discussants. No other book is needed.

Organizing Session

At the first session the group will decide on:

- Form of study
- Number of sessions
- Whether to invite outside experts

- Meeting time and place
- Work assignments

The question of possible study visits to animal clinics etc. may also be taken up for discussion.

Subsequent Sessions

Every session may start with a recapitulation of the previous meeting. Raise and discuss issues that you did not have time to explore or questions provoked by the preceding session.

Introduce the program for the day. The group may take turns doing this as well as recapitulating the previous meeting. Consult the study guide and decide which issues are the most important. Do the questions need complementing on any point?

Do a quick evaluation after every meeting. The leader or one of the members should present the issues to be taken up at the next session.

Introduction

1. The author expresses the hope that "those of you who love your pet may find this book useful and enjoyable — those of you who know that the time to say goodbye will come one day."

   What are you hoping to get out of this study circle? Will you be facing a loss before long? Or do you want to talk about, and thereby work on, a previous loss? Everyone should take turns to explain his or her reasons.

2. Even though those with whom the author has spoken have been mourning, "they have almost always expressed great happiness and gratefulness for the past and have usually said that they are hoping for a new relationship and commitment."

   Have you ever experienced the death of a loved animal? If so, tell about your animal, about your grief and how you were affected.

Losing Someone You Love

3. The author says that grief is a psychological crisis, a "decisive turn, a sudden change, a fatal disturbance." She also claims that "crises in life are necessary to our personal development and increased self-awareness."

   Do you know someone who has experienced a deep grief? How did this crisis affect his or her personality — in a positive or negative way?

4. Grief may entail life-long suffering if the bereaved "gets stuck" and fixed in his sorrow, bitter and incapable of finding a meaning in life. Do you think that knowledge of the nature of grief is able to affect our ability to handle it?

5. Shock is a state of stress in which certain parts of the brain become blocked. You act and think irrationally.

   At the news that a dog is incurably ill or seriously injured most dog owners find themselves in a state of shock. In this state they are sometimes forced to make important decisions.

   The author is telling us never to make important decisions in this state, since chances are that your decisions would be unwise. What should you do? How do you know whether you are in a state of shock? What can your surroundings do to help? Talk about it!

6. A state of shock may last for several weeks. You may be calm and collected outwardly, but inside, all is chaos and panic. Discuss whether you should call in sick and avoid driving during this time, for instance.

7. The reaction and working-through stages mean that what has happened or what lies ahead is beginning to sink in. During this stage, you have all kinds of physical symptoms, such as headaches, loss of appetite, sleeplessness and stomach problems. Have you experienced similar problems?

8. Immediately following the death of your pet you often find it hard to think of anything else. You lack concentration, you are restless and irritable. You may find it hard to concentrate on your daily tasks.

There is not much your surroundings can do to comfort you and ease your pain during that stage, but close friends can be of practical help. In what way? Discuss what those around you can do during this period.

9. Many have the sensation that they can "hear" or "feel" the dead pet close by, even though common sense tells them that the animal is gone forever. Do you think that this feeling of nearness is an expression of our yearning for the dog to return? Or might there be another explanation?

Factors Influencing Grief

10. Many dog owners seem totally unprepared for the fact that their dog will leave them one day. Even the death of an aged dog may come as a complete surprise.

    To what extent do you think it is possible to prepare for the death of a dog? Discuss how you may do this in practical terms.

11. In what way may gender stereotypes, expectations and your social situation affect the grieving process? Give concrete examples.

12. Having a dog, according to Mickie Gustafson, is a complete way of life. What do you think she means by that? What share of your thoughts, feelings and actions do or did you devote to your dog?

13. Discuss the difference between losing a young dog and an old one.

14. How important are farewell rituals to the bereaved? Should there be more pet cemeteries? Is there one in your community?

15. When an animal becomes acutely ill or has an accident, the owner may be helpless. The veterinary clinic may be closed. He or she does not know where to turn or may not have access to a car. There is no ambulance or emergency number to call in a pet emergency. Discuss why this is so and what can be done.

Let Live or Let Die — The Difficult Decision of Mercy Killing

16. Guilt feelings are common on dog owners who have lost their dog. These feelings are often linked to the fact that you have had to make the difficult decision about euthanasia. Discuss whether being able to decide over the life or death of a dog is a good thing.

17. Discuss the statement by Bernie S. Siegel (page 51).

18. Many dog owners worry about the dog getting old and/or becoming ill and incapable of enjoying life.
    What factors are of decisive importance for a dog's quality of life in your opinion? Do certain signs of old age such as diminished hearing or eye sight, stiff joints etc. necessarily mean that the dog no longer enjoys life?

19. In addition to quality of life, there are other factors which affect the decision concerning euthanasia. What might be the practical considerations of caring for an old or infirm dog over a long period of time? The dog has to have medication and maybe a special diet. It is no longer as agile as it used to be. It is no longer able to climb stairs or get into the car without help, etc. Discuss the problem!

20. Do you think that others should be allowed to influence the decision concerning euthanasia, or is this a decision for the dog owner alone? When can those around you be of help? And when are they a hindrance?

21. Which is the best way to prepare for the difficult moment? Why is it wise to be well prepared?

22. Where should the euthanasia take place — at home or at the veterinarian's? Discuss the pros and cons from the dog owner's point of view.

23. Many dog owners find that they experience unexpected inner strength at the difficult moment of their dog's euthanasia. Why do you think that is?

The Role of the Veterinarian

24. Discuss how you would like for the vet to act towards you and towards your dog during euthanasia.

25. Why is it that some veterinarians tend to act too "routinely" when faced with a situation of euthanasia? Discuss the problems they may be encountering.

26. What should the considerations of a veterinarian be in informing an upset dog owner, who may be in a state of shock, of his dog's ill health?

27. There have been instances of a physically healthy dog being condemned for psychological reasons. Who is capable of assessing the mental condition of a dog? Is the vet? What is "bad-tempered"? Discuss possible differences of opinion.

28. What do you think the consequences would be if veterinarians refused to put away young and healthy animals?

29. How can the vet be of help and support to the bereaved?

Managing Your Grief

30. What has your dog meant to you? In what way is the grieving process made easier if you truly acknowledge the emotional and social importance of your dog in your life?

31. Why is it very important to accept and express your grief? What may be the consequences of trying to avoid pain by not permitting yourself to grieve?

32. Everybody accepts and understands when you mourn a person. Not everybody shows the same tolerance for those who mourn a loved animal. How may a lack of understanding among the surroundings affect the grieving process of a pet owner?

33. "Settle your guilt," says the author. What does she mean? What does she want the bereaved to do?

34. How do you know when it is time to conclude the grieving process?

35. In her book *Self-help for your Nerves*, Dr. Claire Weekes says: "Suffering is accompanied by tiredness, and tiredness by more tiredness, for feeling tired makes us exhausted — though it may sound paradoxical!"

    Why do you feel tired and exhausted when things are hard? Discuss the connection between tiredness and our thought patterns. Compare Mickie Gustafson's words about grief-enhancing and destructive thoughts.

36. Discuss the statement by Paul Brunton on page 69.

37. Discuss the meaning of the following: "All of our experiences are enacted and relived in our thoughts."

38. It happens occasionally that the bereaved finds himself unable to work his way through the various stages of grief and gets stuck. What may be the reason for such prolonged grief?

Helping Each Other

39. In *Coming Home*, Deborah Duda tells of a Mexican custom. At the funeral, everyone keeps asking the bereaved how the deceased died. Everybody already knows precisely what happened, but it gives the bereaved a chance to repeat the story over and over. What may be the reason behind such a custom? Do you know of anything similar?

40. Mickie Gustafson claims that the greatest help is just to be there, listening and asking questions. We often find even this difficult. Why do you think that is?

41. Should you show your sympathy by sending flowers, cards etc., or calling — thereby risking that the bereaved will show his or her feelings openly?

42. Why are we so afraid of hurting the bereaved? Why do we shy away from tears and strong emotions?

43. Discuss what you can learn from listening to someone who has lost a close friend.

44. Discuss the conversation between Anneli and Mickie. Are you struck by anything special?

45. Discuss the advice of Lennart Koskinen (page 89–90).

46. Provide some examples of how the emotional ties of children to animals differ from those of adults.

47. Mickie Gustafson states that parents and other adults sometimes underestimate the grief children may experience when they lose a beloved pet. What is she referring to?

48. Why is it important to be honest with children? And why should children, to the extent possible, be allowed to participate in the deliberations and decision about having a pet put away?

49. The author stresses the importance of letting children express their feelings of disappointment, despair, anger etc. Do you think all children will do this spontaneously, or does it sometimes require the assistance of a grownup? If so, how?

50. What is the importance of a funeral or other kind of ceremony associated with the death of the pet for children's ability to manage and work on their grief? Discuss the "rabbit funeral" on page 98!

51. Discuss whether it is possible for children to carry through a constructive grieving process. How may their grieving affect them as adults, both when it comes to managing grief and risking strong emotional attachments?

Grief and Loss from Other Causes

52. Sometimes you have to give up your dog for purely practical reasons, such as allergies, changed working or family circumstances etc. Separation may be made easier by finding a good home for the dog. Even so, many dog owners prefer to have their dog put away, even though it may still be young and have a healthy appetite for life. Discuss why this may be so.

53. If your dog runs away or is stolen, what help in retrieving it can you expect from the authorities?

54. What can the dog owner expect to spend in terms of time and money to recover a lost dog? Discuss whether there should be a

spot on the local radio station or a special column in the newspaper to advertise a lost dog.

55. Could a voluntary separation ever be more painful than losing a dog from natural causes?

Welcoming a New Dog

56. Discuss the disadvantages of getting another dog before the owner has concluded the grieving process for the old one.

57. How do you know whether you are ready to get another dog?

58. What are the reasons why many dog owners get another dog relatively soon after the loss of the old one? What did you do, or what would you do?

59. When is giving a child a cuddly toy animal preferable to a real live animal?

60. Some dog owners acquire a puppy while the aged and ailing dog is still alive. Discuss the wisdom of this.

61. What may adding a puppy to the family mean to an old, tired and possibly severely ill dog? And what does it mean to the pup to grow up in the shadow of an older dog?

62. Some dog owners hasten to get a dog of the same breed, sex and color as the old one, and sometimes even give it the same name. What do you think of this?

Epilogue

63. Various religions contain differing statements and explanations concerning human beings, life and death. But few mention animals. Why is this? What are your thoughts and ideas concerning this?